Far from the Madding Crowd

Thomas Hardy

Guide written and developed by
John Mahoney and Stewart Martin

Charles Letts & Co Ltd
London, Edinburgh & New York

First published 1987
by Charles Letts & Co Ltd
Diary House, Borough Road, London SE1 1DW

Illustration: Peter McClure

The authors gratefully acknowledge the help given to them by 'The Thomas Hardy
Society Limited' in providing source material for the map which appears on p. 8.

Stewart Martin is an Honours graduate of Lancaster University, where he read English
and Sociology. He has worked both in the UK and abroad as a writer, a teacher, and an
educational consultant. He is married with three children, and is currently deputy
headmaster at Ossett School in West Yorkshire.

John Mahoney has taught English for twenty years. He has been head of English
department in three schools and has wide experience of preparing students at all levels
for most examination boards. He has worked both in the UK and North America
producing educational books and computer software on English language and literature.
He is married with three children and lives in Worcestershire.

British Library Cataloguing in Publication Data
Mahoney, John
    Far from the madding crowd: Thomas Hardy:
    guide. – (Guides to literature)
    1. Hardy, Thomas, *1840–1928*. Far from the madding crowd
    I. Title   II. Martin, Stewart   III. Series
    8238.'   PR4745

ISBN 0 85097 768 1

Printed and bound in Great Britain by
Charles Letts (Scotland) Ltd

Contents

To the student

This study companion to your English literature text acts as a guide to the novel or play being studied. It suggests ways in which you can explore content and context, and focuses your attention on those matters which will lead to an understanding, appreciative and sensitive response to the work of literature being studied.

Whilst covering all those aspects dealt with in the traditional-style study aid, more importantly, it is a flexible companion to study, enabling you to organize the patterns of study and priorities which reflect your particular needs at any given moment.

Whilst in many places descriptive, it is never prescriptive, always encouraging a sensitive personal response to a work of literature, rather than the shallow repetition of others' opinions. Such objectives have always been those of the good teacher, and have always assisted the student to gain high grades in 16+ examinations in English literature. These same factors are also relevant to students who are doing coursework in English literature for the purposes of continual assessment.

The major part of this guide is the 'Commentary' where you will find a detailed commentary and analysis of all the important things you should know and study for your examination. There is also a section giving practical help on how to study a set text, write the type of essay that will gain high marks, prepare coursework and a guide to sitting examinations.

Used sensibly, this guide will be invaluable in your studies and help ensure your success in the course.

Thomas Hardy

Thomas Hardy was born in 1840 at the village of Bockhampton, not far from Dorchester, the Casterbridge of the novel. He was encouraged to read by his mother, and from his father he learnt to play the violin, acquiring a love of music which is evident in much of his writing. He was educated at the local village school and later at a private school in Dorchester. He received no university training, an omission which was to cause him much intellectual insecurity.

At the age of sixteen he was apprenticed to an architect in Dorchester and learnt about the restoration of churches and old houses. In his spare time he undertook the study of the Latin and Greek classics. In 1862 he moved to London to work as an architectural assistant, but in 1867 he returned to Bockhampton because of ill-health. His knowledge of architecture can be seen in the detailed descriptions he gives of the buildings of Casterbridge. In 1870 Hardy visited Cornwall to plan the restoration of a church. During the visit he met Emma Lavinia Gifford whom he married in 1874.

Hardy began writing poems, but abandoned this for prose writing. In 1874 he gave up his career as an architect in order to concentrate on writing. Most of his novels were published in serial form for magazines in England and America. He worried that his writing was suffering because of the need to cater for his serial audience.

After his marriage Hardy moved about a great deal, living in Surbiton, Swanage, Yeovil and Sturminster-Newton. In 1883 he returned to Dorchester to supervise the building of his house into which he moved in 1885. Hardy visited London frequently, meeting other famous literary figures. Many of his novels met with severe criticism and the publication of *Jude the Obscure* in 1896 was given such a hostile reception that Hardy gave up writing novels altogether and went back to poetry.

His marriage to Emma Gifford was not particularly successful, but he stayed with her until she died in 1912. Two years later he married a much younger woman, Florence Dugdale, who had been acting as his secretary. After his death in 1928, his heart was removed and buried in the grave of his first wife at Stinsford near Dorchester.

Wessex is the name Hardy gives to his fictional county, taken from the name given to the south-west region of England when it was a Saxon kingdom. Casterbridge is based roughly on mid-century Dorchester. All the towns and villages correspond to real places but are given different names so that over the course of several novels Hardy built up an imaginary world.

Far from the Madding Crowd first appeared in a serialized form in the *Cornhill Magazine* during the period December 1873 to December 1874. It was also published in book form in the November of that year. Its popularity both here and abroad was quickly established.

Whilst some of the characters in this book have connections with those of *The Mayor of Casterbridge*—Bathsheba's uncle, James Everdene, and a much younger Boldwood both make an appearance at the bankruptcy of Mr Henchard, the mayor—the story does not continue to have at its heart the great changes that were occurring during the 19th century. Rather, the traditional rural beliefs, customs and values are presented and explored.

The view of nature as a force indifferent to the plight of man and often malevolent towards him is a theme which runs through *Far from the Madding Crowd*, and the little village of Weatherbury lies largely untouched by the outside forces for social and economic change. What we see here is the unchanging face of nature and the men and women who are in tune with her various ways. Those characters who are not really of the 'rustic mould', Troy, Boldwood and Fanny, die or depart the scene leaving just the two main characters, Bathsheba and Gabriel in harmony with the rural life.

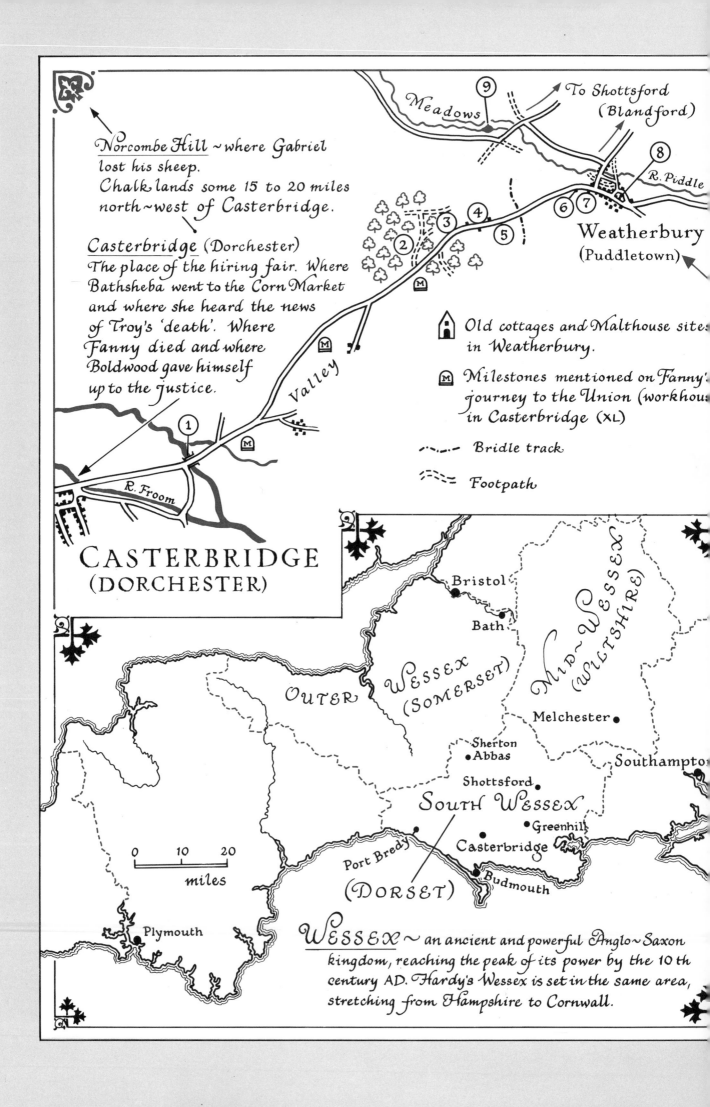

Norcombe Hill ~ where Gabriel
lost his sheep.
Chalk lands some 15 to 20 miles
north~west of Casterbridge.

Casterbridge (Dorchester)
The place of the hiring fair. Where
Bathsheba went to the Corn Market
and where she heard the news
of Troy's 'death'. Where
Fanny died and where
Boldwood gave himself
up to the justice.

Meadows

To Shottsford
(Blandford)

R. Piddle

Weatherbury
(Puddletown)

Old cottages and Malthouse sites
in Weatherbury.

Milestones mentioned on Fanny's
journey to the Union (workhouse)
in Casterbridge (XL)

— · — · — Bridle track

===== ===== Footpath

Valley

R. Froom

CASTERBRIDGE
(DORCHESTER)

Bristol

Bath

OUTER WESSEX (SOMERSET)

MID~WESSEX (WILTSHIRE)

Melchester

Sherton
Abbas

Shottsford

Southampton

SOUTH WESSEX

Greenhill

Casterbridge

0   10   20
miles

Port Bredy

(DORSET)

Budmouth

Plymouth

WESSEX ~ an ancient and powerful Anglo~Saxon
kingdom, reaching the peak of its power by the 10th
century AD. Hardy's Wessex is set in the same area,
stretching from Hampshire to Cornwall.

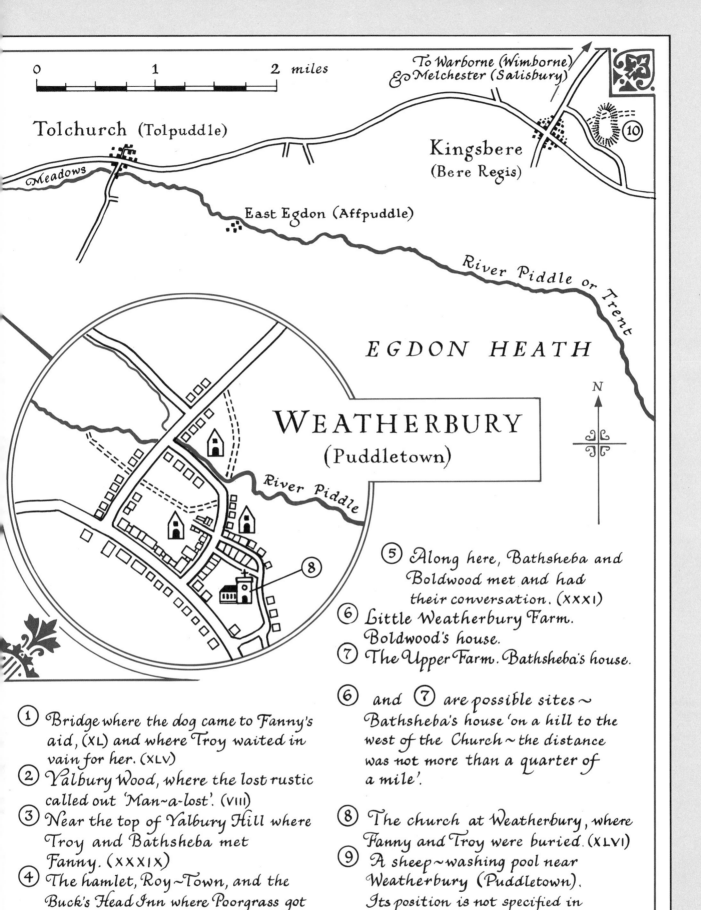

0   1   2 miles

To Warborne (Wimborne)
& Melchester (Salisbury)

Tolchurch (Tolpuddle)

Meadows

Kingsbere
(Bere Regis)

⑩

East Egdon (Affpuddle)

River Piddle or Trent

EGDON HEATH

N

WEATHERBURY
(Puddletown)

River Piddle

⑧

⑤ Along here, Bathsheba and
Boldwood met and had
their conversation. (XXXI)
⑥ Little Weatherbury Farm.
Boldwood's house.
⑦ The Upper Farm. Bathsheba's house.

⑥ and ⑦ are possible sites ~
Bathsheba's house 'on a hill to the
west of the Church ~ the distance
was not more than a quarter of
a mile'.

① Bridge where the dog came to Fanny's
aid, (XL) and where Troy waited in
vain for her. (XLV)
② Yalbury Wood, where the lost rustic
called out 'Man~a~lost'. (VIII)
③ Near the top of Yalbury Hill where
Troy and Bathsheba met
Fanny. (XXXIX)
④ The hamlet, Roy~Town, and the
Buck's Head Inn where Poorgrass got
drunk while taking Fanny's coffin
to Weatherbury. (XLII)

⑧ The church at Weatherbury, where
Fanny and Troy were buried. (XLVI)
⑨ A sheep~washing pool near
Weatherbury (Puddletown).
Its position is not specified in
the novel.
⑩ Greenhill, where the sheep fair
took place ~ and Troy made his
appearance as Turpin.

Peter McClure 1986

Understanding Far from the Madding Crowd

An exploration of the major topics and themes in the novel

Summaries of themes

Nature

Every major scene and incident in the story has as its background, and often as an integral part, the forces of nature. It is depicted as an unrelenting, uncontrollable force with many faces. Its harsh side is shown in incidents like the loss of Gabriel's flock and the storm which might have destroyed the ricks. When characters face despair and disillusion it is often near damp, dark and evil-seeming places which reflect their emotional state. The calm face of nature, its warm spring, summer and harvest, and bright starlit winters are important as they create tone and atmosphere which help to support and interpret the action of the story. Of the five major characters, only two of them are really in tune with their natural environment, Gabriel and Bathsheba. Note especially Gabriel's mental attitudes to the shocks and upsets which afflict him. He is steadfast and dependable, like the oak tree from which he gets his name. Like nature's mighty oak, he survives through all seasons, reflecting the harmony of man when close to nature, wherein all life is rooted.

Landscape and environment
Hardy's description of farm and country landscape, and village life is detailed and perceptive. His early training in architecture is often in evidence when he is describing the man-made structures. His fine impressions of the landscape demonstrate a precision gained through familiarity with the subject.

The seasons
The constant and predictable cycle of the seasons through the year, despite local variations in weather patterns, emphasizes a constancy within the world of nature.

The seasons have great symbolic significance for the experiences and future of the various lovers. It is in winter that Gabriel first proposes to Bathsheba, and is rejected. With the coming of spring we see the beginning of Boldwood's desire, inspired by Bathsheba's thoughtless valentine and fanned by her vanity. Summer sees the heightening of this passion, but it is Troy who wins 'the harvest', with his marriage to Bathsheba in mid-July. As autumn turns to winter so the death of Fanny occurs. As the year draws to its close we see the destruction of both Troy and Boldwood. With the new year Bathsheba faces a new life, values and expectations. For both her and Gabriel there is a new beginning and a time for new growth.

The story begins in December and ends just after December, some four years later. But through all this period it is not so much the passing of hours and minutes that is important, but the slow movement of season passing into season as a background to the playing out of the characters' passions.

Weather
The weather is shown in three ways in the novel: as part of the natural setting, giving tone and life to the changing seasons; as part of the uncontrollable forces of nature or fate as seen in the storm which threatens Bathsheba's ricks and her fortune; lastly as symbolic of the situation, hopes and fate of the characters, as for example, in the rain on Fanny's grave and the sun in Bathsheba's eyes.

Animals
In this story, so closely tied to the rural community, animal life plays its part in linking man and nature and helping to illustrate the nature of work in such a community. The

three major 'sheep' scenes: the destruction of Gabriel's flock, the saving of Bathsheba's flock by Gabriel, and the sheep-shearing where Gabriel and Bathsheba are for a moment joined as in one of the great pastoral paintings which depict the idyll of the countryside, all serve to point up the action of the novel, the characters' emotions, thoughts and desires, and reflect the sympathetic background of the seasons in which they occur. Gabriel's losing and saving a flock illustrates the countryman's acceptance of fate while using learned skills to establish his place in the environment.

Fanny's journey to the workhouse in some ways represents the depths to which man can sink, in that it is left to a dog to help her survive the last faltering steps she takes before her death. Man's reward to the dog, is a hail of stones from the workhouse master. There is a stark contrast here with the inhumanity of 'civilized' man to his fellow beings – note particularly Troy's treatment of all the other main characters.

Structure

The serialization of the story obviously requires the author to bear in mind the needs of his audience, who, at the end of one instalment must be encouraged to purchase the next edition. This is done in a variety of ways: perhaps by an unresolved mystery, a developing relationship the readers wish to see explored, or the introduction of a catastrophe – natural or otherwise. These lead to moments of great suspense in the structure of the novel.

Do note the major 'patterns' which are to be found in the novel and which balance one another in the unfolding of the story. You should have in mind the major 'rustic' conversations and descriptions, the lengthy pastoral scenes and the character descriptions which the author provides. Remember that much of our knowledge of the characters comes not from their actions but in the form of a lengthy comment from the author, but there are also major conversations, almost 'set-pieces', which assist in the portrayal and development of character. For each of these aspects you should be aware of how they interrelate, what precedes and follows them, their content and how they both highlight and act as a sympathetic background to the action of the novel.

Death
Death, as with other images in the novel, can be seen in its natural and timely place and also as an untimely and tragic occurrence.

The death of Gabriel's sheep seems to destroy his hopes of marrying Bathsheba, but ironically sets him on the road to Weatherbury where he will once again meet his love. The death of an old uncle gives Bathsheba her inheritance, initially takes her away from Gabriel but actually ensures that they will meet again. Fanny dies because she is a victim of society, innocence, and ignorance, but her death helps to open Bathsheba's eyes to Troy's true nature. Troy dies in the heat of the moment – exactly fitting to the way he lived but at the hand of a man possessed by an unnatural passion. The imprisonment of Boldwood and the death of Troy leaves the way open for the fulfilment of Gabriel's hopes.

Light and dark
Hardy continually uses the effects of light in his descriptions. This takes on a symbolic importance when light and dark are shown together. Contrasting characters can be seen through the sustained images – Oak illuminates the darkness while Troy dazzles the sight. Use of natural forms of illumination such as the sun, moon or stars contrasts symbolically with artificial ones like lamplight or bright materials. Readers should be aware of the movement of the novel between night and day; almost half of the chapters are set in the evening or night.

Red/flame
It is important to note Hardy's use of these images in connection with Troy – his dazzling red uniform – for these are maintained throughout the novel. In this way the reader sees the evil in Troy not in the black, sombre tones of the power of darkness but as an 'illuminated scarlet'. Hellfire then has a brilliant, attractive side, to which Bathsheba responds and towards which the reader is drawn as well.

The red spot – the seal on the valentine – which so inflamed Boldwood's passions, finds its mirror image in the 'red coat' of Troy which sets Bathsheba on her passionate and downward path.

Time   Time is noted by the passing seasons and recollected by church holidays and Saints' Days. The two watches – important time images – illuminate the perspective of the two owners. Gabriel's timepiece was unreliable but he knows how to read nature's clock, the stars. Troy's watch is elaborate, an heirloom bearing a motto which reads, 'Love and circumstances' and pinpoints the central conflict of the relationships of all the main characters. This then, with the lock of Fanny's hair concealed in Troy's watch, focuses the reader on Troy's lack of concern with times past or present and his desire for momentary gratification.

Character

Flattery   Flattery is the use of language to persuade another by appealing to vanity. Bathsheba is the character most easily swayed by flattery because she enjoys it and therefore is the most vulnerable. It leads her into most painful relationships causing her to reject a worthier man. By the end of the novel she has developed and matured to a point where 'pretty phrases' are unnecessary (chapter 56). Gabriel and Bathsheba will not have a marriage which is based upon romanticism and superficiality.

Independence   The desire for independence is most stressed in the character of Bathsheba. She represents a striving for emancipation and independence from men, who were often far from her equal in assurance, native intelligence and education. Independence is asserted in her appearance in the corn market and management of her farm. The loss of both emotional and social independence is noted in her relationship with Troy. The need for mutual interdependence is seen in her relationship with Gabriel.

Instability   Hardy highlights the unstable aspects of some of his major characters with the stability and rhythm of seasonal country life. Against this backdrop the reader views Bathsheba's instability in her acts of impulsiveness, Troy's lack of personal perspective, and Boldwood's uncontrolled and obsessive passion. All this highlights the reader's understanding of the value and source of Gabriel's stabilizing qualities of endurance and patience.

Name   In this novel Hardy often uses names as a statement about the character, for example 'Oak'. The names of the rustics such as Pennyways and Poorgrass follow this pattern. Note how many of the true rustic characters have biblical names, not least Bathsheba and Gabriel. There is an association here with the pastoral traditions and customs of the Old Testament characters.

Hardy also plays on the idea of identity, by holding the name of the character back from the reader, or from another character in the novel.

Responsibility   Responsibility is centred in the novel in the 'quiet energy' of Gabriel Oak. The personal integrity required to make a responsible human being is highlighted by the contrasting characters and their response to events in the novel. Troy and Bathsheba symbolize the havoc caused by reckless, ill-considered or simply careless actions and Boldwood's sense of responsibility is eaten away by his obsession. The reader is constantly aware of the two-fold nature of responsibility in the rural community – moral responsibility which stabilizes it and practical responsibility by which it survives. An example of this is the irresponsible way in which Troy leads the rustics into a drunken party, ignoring his duties as farmer and husband, whereas Bathsheba recognizes her duty here and pleads that the workers should not be given the strong drink to which they are not accustomed.

Selfishness   Selfishness is illustrated in the characters of Bathsheba and Troy. Bathsheba's selfishness is shown through her emotional immaturity, vanity and fickleness. Troy's brand of selfishness is founded in his irresponsibility toward women and toward others he should care about, for example the farm workers (chapter 36). The ease with which he spends Bathsheba's money is a further example. To some extent, Boldwood shows a great deal of selfishness in that his 'love' for Bathsheba is more centred on the satisfaction of his own desires than on the needs of Bathsheba.

Vanity   Vanity is a selfish quality which creates vulnerability in a character. Bathsheba's vanity is clarified in the reader's first view of her. In this way she undervalues Gabriel because he does not appeal to her vanity through words, it opens her to Troy's insincere appeal, and leads to disaster with Boldwood through her wish to gain the attention of a man who seems disinterested in her.

The rural community

The rustics Depth and strength are added to the novel through the characterization of the rustics. They represent the rituals, ways and work of an agricultural community. Hardy's novel is not concerned with the real hardships commonly experienced by Victorian agricultural workers but more with their symbolic presence in a world soon to change with the growth of technology and industry. His description of them centres upon their individuality, humour, warmth, wit and language, which places them in a comfortable coexistence in the natural world. The rustics can be seen to offer comic relief in a novel of otherwise somewhat sombre and occasionally melodramatic tones, for example when Fanny's coffin is delayed by more pressing matters thus giving us the ironic picture of a woman late not only for her wedding but also for her funeral!

The rustics do not figure in the central action though they are an essential thread running through the fabric of the novel. They counterpoint, link, and comment upon the major aspects of the novel.

Rural life is the essence of the novel. Against this backdrop of country life, customs, work, celebrations and natural disasters, the action takes place, the characters unfold and the plot works itself out.

Music Music is part of the fabric of Victorian country life, and in the novel provides some of the most moving moments. Music adds to the farm workers' life in their celebrations, for example the harvest supper; in easing the hardships, for example Gabriel at the hiring fair; and as a natural way of communicating their emotions – ranging from humour to sadness in the words of their songs. The bringing of music to the final scene is a fine example of the harmonious power of music in rural communities.

Setting Wessex was not just a physical location to Hardy, it encompassed a social and economic order with customs, a life-style and inhabitants which Hardy loved and sought to preserve through his novels. *Far from the Madding Crowd* was the first of the Wessex novels.

Status and social position The Victorian social structure is depicted in a natural way in this country setting where each has his job and his natural place. Outside this stands Troy, a military man of an interesting background. Boldwood is a man in a respected position who surprises the readers when he shows unexpected weakness of character. Gabriel is a man so in harmony with his natural place in the order of life that he is able to accept his fate even when Bathsheba seems to have risen beyond his grasp. Bathsheba is interesting because she represents the 'new woman' in society, independent and determined to run her own life. She is attracted by her own new-found status and by the possibility of reinforcing this through marriage to Boldwood, but these considerations play no part in her decision to marry Troy.

With the picture of Fanny, a working-class girl, victim of simple love and irresponsibility, Hardy comments on the plight of women in society, a theme he explored fully in his later novel, *Tess of the D'Urbervilles*.

Love and marriage

Love Hardy's novel clearly defines the positive and negative forces of love. Oak's love is enduring, reliable, and above all based upon a realistic view of the loved one. Bathsheba rejects Gabriel because she does not 'love' him and her actions in the first part of the novel display her innocence of men, love and desire. In Fanny we see the victim of love; innocent in a different way from Bathsheba, she is totally unable to cope with a man like Troy. Boldwood symbolizes the destructive nature of obsessive love, a love which destroys him and comes close to doing the same to Bathsheba. In Troy we see the face of arrogant romanticism which is appealing in its spontaneity but is destructive in its fickleness and its lack of endurance. By the end of the novel Bathsheba has learned through painful experience the value of Gabriel's ability to love her through all adversity. They are 'such tried good friends'.

Marriage

Marriage is one of the major themes of the novel and certainly the central concern of the main characters. Hardy considers in this novel the reasons for and the impact of marriage on his particular choice of characters. Their reasons for proposal, rejection or acceptance are personalized and are not intended to be representative of a certain trait in society. What the theme of marriage does is to provide a framework for Bathsheba's development; her suitors' actions test her poise, independence, recklessness, conflicts and final maturity.

The destructive power of sexuality is highlighted by Bathsheba's innocence in the early part of the novel and the difficulty she has in controlling these situations with her husband and with Boldwood in the later chapters.

Boldwood's obsessional love is a major example of the havoc caused by desire. Can you think of others?

Fate and irony

Fate

Fate in the form of chance and coincidence creates many of the circumstances in which the characters find themselves. A distinction is drawn between the characters who are directed by chance, like Boldwood, and those who make an effort to change circumstances and learn by misfortune, like Gabriel. Fate takes control of events in Bathsheba's life at the time when she plays a game of finding a husband in the chance fall of a book. She finds there is no way she can escape from the circumstances this leads to. Fanny's fate is sealed when she muddles the church names and misses the wedding. Troy curses fate and turns his back on it at Fanny's spoiled grave. Gabriel's strength and sense of a wider meaning of life enable him to overcome disasters and re-order his life.

Irony

The catastrophic loss of Gabriel's sheep destroys his fortune but also makes a new fortune possible. A mere lock of hair helps lead to Troy's downfall. The comment near the start of the novel which refers to a woman needing a disaster to bring out the best in her finds its ironic fulfilment in the disaster which befalls Bathsheba at the end and finds her rising to the occasion. These and many other events and comments help provide links between various aspects of the plot and characterization. Much of it is drawn to your attention in the commentary, but do also look out for the many examples which are not mentioned.

Analysis chart

Dates	1	2	3	4	5	6	7	8	9	10	11	12	13	14	15	16	17	18	19	20	21	22	23	24
Dates	Year 1: December		27 December			Year 2: February							13 February					April		Early spring		1 June		
Chapter	1	2	3	4	5	6	7	8	9	10	11	12	13	14	15	16	17	18	19	20	21	22	23	24
Important events	Gabriel first sees Bathsheba	Bathsheba rescues Gabriel from suffocation	Gabriel proposes to Bathsheba		Gabriel's sheep killed. Bathsheba goes to Weatherbury	Gabriel helps put out fire on Bathsheba's rick	Gabriel meets Fanny				Troy promises to marry Fanny		Bathsheba sends valentine to Boldwood		Boldwood learns that Bathsheba sent valentine	Fanny 'misses' her marriage			The 'sheep washing'. Boldwood proposes to Bathsheba	Gabriel dismissed	Gabriel re-employed		Sheep-shearing supper	Bathsheba first meets Troy
Places Weatherbury						●	●	●	●	●		●	●	●	●			●	●	●	●	●	●	●
Casterbridge						●						●					●							
Road to Casterbridge																								
Norcombe	●	●	●	●	●																			
Melchester											●				●									
Greenhill Fair																								
Characters Bathsheba	●		●	●		●	●	●	●	●		●	●	●	●			●	●	●	●	●	●	●
Gabriel Oak	●	●	●	●	●	●	●	●	●	●			●	●				●	●	●	●	●	●	●
Mr Boldwood			●						●			●	●	●	●			●	●	●	●		●	●
Sergeant Troy			●								●				●	●								●
Fanny Robin							●	●	●	●	●				●	●								
Themes Nature	●	●			●			●			●			●				●	●			●		●
Structure	●	●			●	●		●			●			●	●		●						●	●
Characters	●	●	●	●	●	●	●	●	●	●		●			●			●	●			●	●	●
The rural community						●		●	●	●					●					●	●	●	●	
Love and marriage			●						●				●						●	●		●		●
Fate and irony			●			●				●			●	●		●							●	●
Page in commentary on which chapter first appears	21	23	24	25	27	27	29	29	31	31	32	33	34	34	35	36	36	37	37	38	39	41	42	42

25	26	27	28	29	30	31	32	33	34	35	36	37	38	39	40	41	42	43	44	45	46	47	48	49	50	51	52	53	54	55	56	57
		Late June						17 July			Late August				9 October								Year 3	September				Christmas Eve		Year 4: March	26 December	

Events (by chapter):

- 27 — Troy hives the bees
- 28 — Troy displays his skill with a sword
- 33 — Bathsheba and Troy married
- 36 — Harvest supper. Troy and rustics get drunk
- 37 — Gabriel saves ricks from storm
- 39 — Bathsheba and Troy meet Fanny
- 40 — Fanny dies
- 41 — News of Fanny's death
- 43 — Bathsheba opens Fanny's coffin
- 45 — Troy plants flowers on Fanny's grave
- 47 — Troy 'drowns' at Budmouth
- 48 — News of Troy's 'death'
- 49 — Sheep fair at Greenhill. Troy returns
- 53 — Boldwood's party. Troy shot
- 54 — Boldwood tried
- 56 — Gabriel tells Bathsheba he will emigrate
- 57 — Gabriel and Bathsheba marry

43	44	44	45	46	46	47	48	49	49	50	51	52	52	53	53	54	55	55	56	57	57	57	58	58	58	59	59	60	61	61	61	62

Finding your way around the commentary

Each page of the commentary gives the following information:

1 A quotation from the start of each paragraph on which a comment is made, or act/scene or line numbers plus a quotation, so that you can easily locate the right place in your text.

2 A series of comments, explaining, interpreting, and drawing your attention to important incidents, characters and aspects of the text.

3 For each comment, headings to indicate the important characters, themes, and ideas dealt with in the comment.

4 For each heading, a note of the comment numbers in this guide where the previous or next comment dealing with that heading occurred.

Thus you can use this commentary section in a number of ways.

1 Turn to that part of the commentary dealing with the chapter/act you are perhaps revising for a class discussion or essay. Read through the comments in sequence, referring all the time to the text, which you should have open before you. The comments will direct your attention to all the important things of which you should take note.

2 Take a single character or topic from the list on page 19. Note the comment number next to it. Turn to that comment in this guide, where you will find the first of a number of comments on your chosen topic. Study it, and the appropriate part of your text to which it will direct you. Note the comment number in this guide where the next comment for your topic occurs and turn to it when you are ready. Thus, you can follow one topic right through your text. If you have an essay to write on a particular character or theme just follow the path through this guide and you will soon find everything you need to know!

3 A number of relevant relationships between characters and topics are listed on page 19. To follow these relationships throughout your text, turn to the comment indicated. As the previous and next comment are printed at the side of each page in the commentary, it is a simple matter to flick through the pages to find the previous or next occurrence of the relationship in which you are interested.

For example, you want to examine in depth the rural community of the novel. Turning to the single topic list, you will find that the 'Rural community' first occurs in comment 52. On turning to comment 52 you will discover a zero (0) in the place of the previous reference (because this is the first time that it has occurred) and the number 61 for the next reference. You now turn to comment 61 and find that the previous comment number is 52 (from where you have just been looking) and that the next reference is to comment 62, and so on throughout the text.

You also wish to trace the relationship between Bathsheba and Boldwood throughout the novel. From the relationships list, you are directed to comment 76. This is the first time that both Bathsheba and Boldwood are discussed together and you will find that the next time that this happens occurs in comment 77 (the 'next' reference for both Bathsheba and Boldwood). On to comment 77 and you will now discover that two different comment numbers are given for the subject under examination – numbers 78 and 45. This is because each character is traced separately as well as together and you will have to continue tracing them separately until you finally come to comment 95 – the next occasion on which both Bathsheba and Boldwood are discussed.

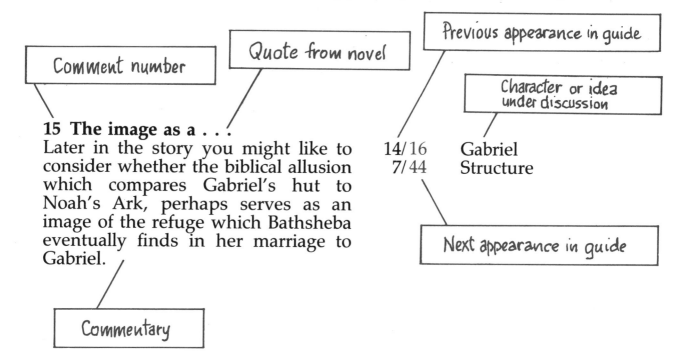

Comment number

Quote from novel

Previous appearance in guide

Character or idea under discussion

Next appearance in guide

Commentary

15 The image as a . . .
Later in the story you might like to consider whether the biblical allusion which compares Gabriel's hut to Noah's Ark, perhaps serves as an image of the refuge which Bathsheba eventually finds in her marriage to Gabriel.

14/16   Gabriel
7/44   Structure

Single topics:

	Comment no:		Comment no:
Nature	4	Bathsheba	7
Structure	3	Mr Boldwood	37
Character	1	Gabriel Oak	1
The rural community	52	Sergeant Troy	25
Love and marriage	31	Fanny Robbin	57
Fate and irony	43		

Relationships:

			Comment no:
Bathsheba	and	Gabriel Oak	12
	and	Mr Boldwood	76
	and	Sergeant Troy	25
	and	Fanny	77
	and	Character	38
	and	Love and marriage	38
Gabriel Oak	and	Mr Boldwood	37
	and	Troy	25
	and	Fanny	57
	and	Character	1
	and	Nature	4
	and	Rural community	62
Mr Boldwood	and	Sergeant Troy	37
	and	Love and marriage	102
	and	Fate and irony	100
	and	Character	76
Sergeant Troy	and	Fanny	88
	and	Love and marriage	166
	and	Character	89

Commentary

Chapter 1

1 When Farmer Oak . . .
It is no accident that Farmer Oak is named as he is. As you read the novel be
aware of his durability and strength, and note how characteristic they are,
both of the oak tree and Farmer Oak. In this name we also see the
juxtaposition of man and nature. It is a feature of the novel that the drama
will be played out against nature's background, a background which is part
and parcel of life at Weatherbury.

0/2	Gabriel
0/2	Character

2 His Christian name . . .
At the end of the last paragraph we were given the image of Farmer Oak's
wrinkles as 'like the rays . . . of the rising sun'. In his Christian name we see
reflected the great strength, patience and goodness of the man, which will
support him and withstand the trials that are to come his way. You will
notice as you read the novel the many references to biblical characters and
events, and the references to classical literature and figures. Gabriel was one
of God's chief angels, sometimes regarded as the angel of death and the
prince of fire and thunder – you might remember these latter two titles when
you read chapter 37. The Mohammedans regard him as the spirit of truth
and other religions view the angel Gabriel in a similar light.

1/3	Gabriel
1/3	Character

3 His Christian name . . .
Note at the bottom of this paragraph how Gabriel's 'character . . . stood in
the scale of public opinion'. Is it he who changes, or his friends and critics in
their tantrums? It is worth noting here what the author is telling us about
Gabriel. His character, attitudes, dress etc, are all seen in telling detail
through the author's eyes. There are other occasions in the book when we
are able to judge Gabriel for ourselves by his actions and words, but much of
what we learn is through the voice of the author.

2/4	Gabriel
2/7	Character
0/7	Structure

4 Since he lived . . .
Note how this paragraph re-emphasizes the durability of Gabriel in the
description of his manner of dress – 'any weaknesses' being compensated for
by 'unstinted dimensions and solidity'. You would do well to always bear in
mind these impressions that we are getting of Gabriel's characteristics. Like
nature, he is not easily moved. The trials and tribulations of life will rage
around him and to an extent affect him, but like his natural surroundings he
will survive the ravages of time and still be there at the end, beaten but not
bowed, and ready to continue his life, just as the countryside will still be
there after the ravages of storms.

3/5	Gabriel
0/5	Nature

5 Mr Oak carried . . .
The reference to Gabriel's 'watch' is interesting. Note it is only really useful
for telling the minutes. Gabriel's life is ruled by a much slower and majestic
timepiece – nature's. Indeed the whole story follows the rhythms of living in

4/6	Gabriel
3/7	Structure
4/13	Nature

the countryside where the rising and setting of the sun, the passing of seasons, and the uncertainties of the weather are the masters of time and man. How do Troy's and Mr Boldwood's watches compare with Gabriel's? Do they help to tell us about their owners in any way?

6 He had just reached . . .
Gabriel's intellect and emotions 'were clearly separated'. As you read the story you might like to consider the extent to which this separation of intellect and emotion helps protect Gabriel against the tribulations he will have to face. Equally, consider whether if he had been perhaps less stolid and more emotional he might have won his heart's desire a little earlier? Certainly you should contrast his emotional stability with that of Mr Boldwood, and the calculating though sometimes unpredictable Sergeant Troy.

5/11   Gabriel

7 The handsome girl . . .
Hardy introduces us to Bathsheba, secretively admiring herself in a mirror. You will need to consider later whether or not this vanity of hers is a very great fault in her character. There is a great deal of peering through windows and looking in mirrors in the course of the story. See if you notice the characters most involved and if it throws much light on them.

0/8   Bathsheba
3/12   Character
5/15   Structure

8 It was a fine . . .
Is Bathsheba attracted to bright colours? Notice how the sun turns her crimson jacket into a 'scarlet glow'. Is there an implied comment on her character here which, along with her vanity, does not promise well for the future? Who else wears a red-coloured jacket in the story?

7/9   Bathsheba

9 The change from . . .
To what extent would you consider 'Woman's prescriptive infirmity' to be a key to much of the novel's events? To which of Bathsheba's character traits do you think this refers? (Don't forget to check 'Background' and her character summary if you are not sure.) You ought to consider how much of the anguish suffered by the three main male characters in the novel – and Bathsheba herself – is caused by this 'infirmity'. Note the prophetic nature of the phrases 'dramas in which men would play a part' and 'hearts . . . lost and won' in connection with this.

8/10   Bathsheba

10 Oak looked from . . .
The dispute over twopence was, in Gabriel's mind, not really worth the effort, it being such a small sum. His opinion was sharply demonstrated to the disputants when he stepped forward and paid the amount himself. What do we learn here about both Bathsheba's and Gabriel's characters?

9/12   Bathsheba

11 Gabriel's features adhered . . .
The exact balance which Gabriel's features demonstrate finds its expression in a biblical allusion. But so balanced is he that Bathsheba gives him hardly a glance, concerned only that he had 'lost her her point'.

6/12   Gabriel

12 Gabriel, perhaps a little . . .
Notice the final word of chapter 1, 'vanity'. In this first chapter Hardy has established some of the characteristics of two of the main characters and whetted our appetites for the resolution of the relationship between this solid citizen, Oak, and this vain and seemingly mean girl.

10/22	Bathsheba
7/17	Character
11/13	Gabriel

Chapter 2

13 It was nearly . . .
This is the first of what will be many detailed descriptions of the countryside which provides the background to the events of the story. Note the emphasis here on the desolate nature of winter, 'decaying', 'blasts', 'smote', 'weakening moan', 'dead multitude'. At the beginning of the chapter mention is made of the 'desolating wind', a wind which later on will be part of the reason why Gabriel almost suffocates and his sheep are lost.

12/14	Gabriel
5/14	Nature

14 Between this half-wooded . . .
There is a contrast between the sounds here created by the wind, and those created by Gabriel on his flute – as mentioned three paragraphs on. The sounds that come from Gabriel's 'Ark' are to be found 'nowhere in the wind' or nature. Do they, like the image of the 'Ark' represent the peace and purity that are part and parcel of Gabriel's character?

13/15	Gabriel
13/17	Nature

15 The image as a . . .
Later in the story you might like to consider whether the biblical allusion which compares Gabriel's hut to Noah's Ark, perhaps serves as an image of the refuge which Bathsheba eventually finds in her marriage to Gabriel.

14/16	Gabriel
7/44	Structure

16 It was only latterly . . .
This quick sketch by the author explains the background to Gabriel's current position. The great patriarchs of the Bible were all shepherds, whose wealth was measured by the size of their flocks.

15/17	Gabriel

17 Oak's motions, though . . .
Note how 'his special power, morally, physically and mentally, was static, owing little or nothing to momentum as a rule'. This is the root of Gabriel's ability to stand alone from the crowd. He is the novel's example of man being part of the greater forces linking all living things with nature. Like nature, he has something of a timelessness about him which will eventually overcome all those problems which he is to meet.

12/22	Character
16/18	Gabriel
14/18	Nature

18 The lamb, revived . . .
Gabriel hardly seems to need the watch he consults. He spends more time studying the stars to ascertain the time of the night, obviously placing more reliance on his judgment there than on the accuracy of his watch. Notice the images at work here which have Gabriel as their pivot. The paragraph before gave a detailed description of the many contents of Gabriel's earthly ark, now we move on to a consideration of the glories of the winter sky and its stars. Between the two stands Gabriel, at his feet the lamb he recently revived, and its mother. How well does this scene serve as an example of the suggestions made in the previous comments?

17/19	Gabriel
17/19	Nature

19 Being a man not . . .
In the face of the work of art that Gabriel now views, 'Human shapes, interferences, troubles, and joys were all as if they were not'. Certainly this is true as far as nature is concerned. To what extent shall we also see a largely similar view reflected in the way that Gabriel deals with life's problems and joys?

18/20   Gabriel
18/47   Nature

20 Farmer Oak went . . .
Gabriel 'spies' on the scene in the hut. This is the second time that Bathsheba is studied by Gabriel, unbeknown to her. It will happen again. Is Gabriel always privy to the 'secrets' of many of the main characters?

19/21   Gabriel

21 Oak, upon hearing . . .
Here we have our first indication that Gabriel wants to marry. What do we know of his requirements in a wife?

20/23   Gabriel

Chapter 3

22 She came up . . .
Again Bathsheba is 'spied' upon by Gabriel. Her ride expresses her joy in the environment, an independence of spirit and unconventional behaviour. Note how she again checks to see that no one is watching her. What is she worried about?

12/23   Bathsheba
17/26   Character

23 That the girl's thoughts . . .
What is it about their characters that in this first face to face encounter it is 'the man who blushed, the maid not at all'? You might like to note those many occasions which occur in the story where characters are described blushing. Which are most affected and does the fact of blushing say anything?

22/24   Bathsheba
21/25   Gabriel

24 A perception caused him . . .
Now it is Bathsheba's turn to blush. Should Gabriel have been more perceptive and not mentioned the fact of his seeing Bathsheba's ride? Certainly, by the way she checked to see if anyone was watching she had not wanted her actions seen. Note the different effect this encounter has on both of them, as outlined three paragraphs on in the novel.

23/25   Bathsheba

25 On opening his eyes . . .
Gabriel, revived by Bathsheba, awakes to find his head cradled in her lap. Much later in the novel she will cradle another man's head in her lap, but have no success in reviving him.

24/27   Bathsheba
23/27   Gabriel
0/37   Troy

26 'Yes, I suppose I . . .'
Note how both Gabriel, and Bathsheba some paragraphs on, shy away from talking about their meeting. Gabriel feels unable to convey his emotion in the 'coarse meshes of language', and Bathsheba is unwilling to be involved in talk that should 'harmonize with the dignity of such a deed'. Why is this?

22/30   Character

27 'I should think . . .'
What do you think might be in Gabriel's mind when he observes 'you might soon get a new one'?

25/28   Gabriel
25/28   Bathsheba

28 She hesitated, somewhat . . .
Is Bathsheba just teasing Gabriel in the way she lets him hold her hand and then suggesting he will want to kiss it? Notice his 'but I will–'. Was he going to say 'if you want me to'? Note their different reactions to this whole incident–which could have ended fatally for Gabriel if Bathsheba had not arrived on the scene.

27/30   Bathsheba
27/29   Gabriel

Chapter 4

29 Love being an extremely . . .
Is there something both comic and perhaps self-denigrating in the way Gabriel compares his desire to see Bathsheba with the same intensity that his dog awaited his meal?

28/31   Gabriel

30 By making inquiries . . . .
We discover, at last, Bathsheba's name. In the Bible, Bathsheba committed adultery with David, later marrying him after he had her husband killed. There is no suggestion of an exact parallel in her relationship with Gabriel, except insofar as Gabriel does marry her after her husband has been killed by a man with whom she had unwittingly agreed to an 'adulterous' marriage. Certainly, like Oak, there are also suggestions in her surname of those timeless qualities of nature which form the backdrop to this story.

28/35   Bathsheba
26/35   Character

31 At last the eighth . . .
Note Gabriel's views on love and marriage, and what they tell us of his character. 'Love is a possible strength in actual weakness' is a phrase that could be applied to other characters–to whom?

29/32   Gabriel
0/38   Love and
        marriage

32 He had made a toilet . . .
Everything about Gabriel reflects the communion he has with nature, even to his waistcoat, 'patterned all over with . . . the beauties of both rose and lily'.

31/33   Gabriel

33 'Yes, I will wait, . . .'
Notice the abruptness with which Gabriel declares his intention to ask Bathsheba to marry him, and the almost crude way in which he asks if she has 'got any other young man hanging about her'. Yet on the other hand the directness and sensibleness of his questions are quite disarming. He appears to give up his quest very easily, and even disparage the whole affair–'that was all I came about . . . I'll take myself off home-along'. For a man who waited on seeing Bathsheba as keenly as his dog awaited his dinner, he is remarkably calm about this rebuff to his desires. Or is his desire more that of infatuation than love?

32/34   Gabriel

34 A man has advanced . . .
Is Gabriel being too presumptive – 'When we be married'? Or has Bathsheba really led him to believe that she will marry him, if not in so many words? Bear in mind her comment 'I never said I was . . .', there are echoes of it in her dealings with Boldwood and Troy later in the novel.

33/37	Gabriel

35 'Why, Farmer Oak,' . . .
Notice how one of Bathsheba's main faults is revealed as she acts without considering the effect of her actions. She asks for time to consider his proposal; again we will see the same request later in the novel when she responds to Boldwood and Troy. Are her reactions to each situation prompted by the same or different emotions?

30/36	Bathsheba
30/36	Character

36 'What I meant . . .'
Note the independence Bathsheba reveals when she declares 'I hate to be thought of as men's property'.

35/38	Bathsheba
35/38	Character

37 'I can make you happy,' . . .
Gabriel outlines the means by which he will make Bathsheba happy. What, if anything, do Boldwood and Troy offer? Bathsheba will actually 'get' these things that she is presently offered, but without Gabriel's help. Note who provides them as you read the story, and see if they actually amount to much. Will what she finally gets from Gabriel amount to much more?

0/76	Boldwood
34/38	Gabriel
25/88	Troy

38 'Well what I mean is . . .'
Consider Gabriel's offer of marriage and Bathsheba's reasons for refusal. What differences between their characters are highlighted? Are the suggestions made earlier that Bathsheba is vain born out here? Note the phrases Gabriel uses, 'a terrible wooden story . . . can say stupider than'. Despite his protestations of love, these phrases are hardly calculated to endear him to Bathsheba.

36/39	Bathsheba
36/46	Character
37/39	Gabriel
31/43	Love and marriage

39 'But I love you . . .'
The proposition that Gabriel would be content only to be liked foreshadows a similar proposal to Bathsheba from Boldwood. There is indeed much of this present conversation which finds a replication in later scenes.

38/41	Bathsheba
38/40	Gabriel

40 'Never,' said Mr Oak . . .
Note the prophetic declaration of love that Gabriel now makes. It foreshadows similar declarations by other characters, but Oak has the firmness of purpose and stability in his character that others lack, and will carry through the promise to its conclusion.

39/42	Gabriel

41 'It seems dreadfully wrong . . .'
Whose making is the 'moral dilemma' in which Bathsheba finds herself? She says she is too independent and would need someone to 'tame' her. Her independent spirit is plain enough and it will lead her into some difficult situations, but exactly what aspect of her character do you think needs to be 'tamed'?

39/43	Bathsheba

42 Farmer Oak had . . .
Note the irony here. His honesty and humility, amongst other things, lead him to lose Bathsheba's hand. But in the long term, what are the very things that impress her about him and largely lead to their reconciliation and marriage?

43 No man likes . . .
Gabriel does ask again, but here, as mentioned near the end of chapter 56, they are beginning to know the 'rougher sides of each other's character'.

Chapter 5

44 The news which . . .
Consider the quiet certainty of Gabriel's attitude to Bathsheba's disappearance. Her going has merely lead to Gabriel's 'flame' for her burning more finely. But with her going comes the necessity for some action which will develop the plot.

45 One night, when Farmer . . .
A little while before a carelessness on Gabriel's part in not opening the ventilation shutters on his ark, brought Bathsheba to him. Now, another carelessness on his part leaves his young dog, already described as being 'so wrong-headed', unsupervised and within sight of his sheep. These are two rather disastrous mistakes for an experienced shepherd to make. Note how it is in the evening that disastrous events often have their origin.

46 Oak was an intensely . . .
Note the sympathy that Gabriel feels for the ewes and their unborn lambs, to be overtaken a few moments later by the realization that he was not insured and was therefore now bankrupt. Typically, however, the nature of the man reasserts itself and he feels relief that he has no wife who would have to share in the poverty 'now coming upon me'. How well the promise contained in the earlier descriptions of Gabriel and his association with the timelessness of nature is fulfilled in his reactions to the loss of his livelihood.

47 Oak raised his head . . .
The images of death surrounding the pool perfectly reflect the tragedy suffered by Gabriel. At a later stage in the novel, Bathsheba will overlook a pool similarly charged with a deathlike atmosphere – do you know the circumstances?

Chapter 6

48 At one end of . . .
The hiring fair, an integral part of the county scene, where men anxiously try to sell their services to the farmers, would perhaps have left lesser men than Gabriel feeling humiliated and sorry for themselves. Note Gabriel's reaction.

His superior appearance leads other men to address him as 'Sir'. He felt a 'dignified calm' and an 'indifference to fate'. His 'abasement had been an exaltation' and his 'loss gain'. Failing to gain employment as a bailiff he adopts the dress of a shepherd, only to be rebuffed again.

49 This reply invariably . . .
Note the irony of the assumption that Gabriel was 'too good to be trustworthy'.

48/50	Gabriel

50 He drew out his flute . . .
Gabriel's ability to overcome hard times is well illustrated in his flute playing. Note how he managed to play with 'Arcadian sweetness' as though he had never known a moment's sorrow.

43/83	Fate and irony
49/53	Gabriel

51 'She's a very vain . . .'
The reader is left in little doubt that the woman the two rustics are talking about must be Bathsheba. Her vanity in constantly regarding herself in the mirror – as on our first acquaintance with her – is well reported by these two men.

32/52	Bathsheba
46/52	Character

52 'And 'a can play . . .'
Notice how the playing of a piano seems to be included in the men's estimation of Bathsheba's vanity – despite her enjoyment of the music. This was one of the things Gabriel offered Bathsheba when he proposed. She needed no help from Gabriel to acquire it.

51/55	Bathsheba
51/56	Character
0/61	Rural community

53 He turned to an opening . . .
It was a catastrophe that drove Gabriel in the general direction of Weatherbury. It is another that leads him directly to Bathsheba. Both occurred at night time.

50/54	Gabriel
47/71	Structure

54 This before Gabriel's eyes . . .
Hardy's description of the light and colour of the rick fire help inject the vitality of action into the scene. Gabriel takes charge, showing himself to be as much the man of action as any other about the place, but more commanding and sensible than those around him. Here, Gabriel saves Bathsheba's ricks from fire, and gains employment as a result. Later he will save her ricks from another element, water, when again the man properly responsible for their safekeeping is 'unable' to do so. What will be Gabriel's reward then?

53/55	Gabriel

55 'Do you want a shepherd . . .'
Is there a prophetic irony in Gabriel's words? Does Bathsheba indeed need a shepherd, not just to see to her sheep but also to look after her? Given our knowledge of Bathsheba to date, how fair do you think is the reference to her as Gabriel's 'cold-hearted darling'?

52/56	Bathsheba
54/57	Gabriel

Chapter 7

<table>
<tr><td></td><td></td></tr>
</table>

56 Bathsheba withdrew into . . .
Note the mixed reactions she has to Gabriel's reappearance and his obvious change of fortune. A page or so further on we learn how Gabriel is astonished to see how the 'unpractised girl' had developed into a 'supervising and cool woman'. To what extent do you think his conclusion that some women only needed an emergency to make them fit to handle it was true in Bathsheba's case?

| 55/68 | Bathsheba |
| 52/61 | Character |

57 Obliged to some . . .
This meeting with Fanny, late in the evening, so soon after the encounter with Bathsheba introduces a note of mystery and suspense into the story, especially with the reference to her voice – 'the low dulcet note suggestive of romance'.

| 55/58 | Gabriel |
| 0/59 | Fanny |

58 'Only a shepherd,' . . .
Is there a suggestion here that, like a beaten man, Gabriel has decided to accept the lot that fate has cast his way?

| 57/59 | Gabriel |

59 She extended her hand . . .
Note how the chance meeting with this young woman, the hint of romance in her voice, the 'throb of tragic intensity', the image of a lamb 'overdriven', all combine to create an air of mystery, suspense and impending tragedy involving this mysterious stranger.

| 58/60 | Gabriel |
| 57/60 | Fanny |

60 The young girl remained . . .
Notice how Gabriel's instincts and Hardy's imagery – 'the penumbra of a very deep tragedy', foreshadow events to come.

| 59/72 | Fanny |
| 59/62 | Gabriel |

Chapter 8

61 Warren's Malthouse was . . .
This is the first of a number of long and detailed 'rustic conversations'. Do not skip over them. A close study of them reveals how well in tune these people are with the natural world through which they earn their livelihood. Hardy demonstrates his familiarity with the lives they lead, but do be aware that this is a somewhat idealized picture of rural life, and much is left unsaid about the hardness of their lives and the cruel suffering that the English peasant experienced. Note the biblical emphasis in the majority of their names which reflects a key element in the ordering of their lives.

56/76	Character
47/66	Nature
52/62	Rural community

62 'That's never Gable Oak's . . .'
The smallness of the world they live in is reflected in the maltster's immediate recounting of his knowledge of Gabriel's forbears. The apparently long lives they lead, 'a young man about sixty-five', 'Billy, a child of forty', put us in mind of the Bible's long-lived patriarchs.

| 60/64 | Gabriel |
| 61/63 | Rural community |

63 'Ay – the other . . .'
Note the religious allusions here, the 'Purification Day' and in the next paragraph the 'God-forgive-me'. The influence of religion and the awesomeness of nature are central to the conduct of their lives.

| 62/64 | Rural community |

64 'No—not at all,' . . .
Note how Gabriel gains immediate acceptance amongst the group of rustics in the malthouse. He is recognized as being one of them.

62/67	Gabriel
63/65	Rural community

65 'True, true; it can't be . . .'
Notice how Hardy describes each rustic character in detail, noting his particular trait. By paying close attention to the description given, we can gradually build up a detailed picture of many of the rustic characters, enabling us to more fully appreciate the clarity of Hardy's view of the community he is drawing for us.

64/66	Rural community

66 'Yes,' continued Joseph . . .
Is there something peculiarly honest, rustic and natural implied in this continual reference to the propensity of many of the characters to blush so much?

61/85	Nature
65/85	Rural community

67 Gabriel broke the silence . . .
Note the confirmation here that Bathsheba is still the 'innermost subject' of Gabriel's heart.

64/71	Gabriel

68 'And did any of . . .'
As with Gabriel, the rustics' long memories enable them to talk about the Everdene family history, thus firmly placing Bathsheba in the same rural background as Gabriel.

56/71	Bathsheba
66/69	Rural community

69 'Well, now, you'd . . .'
There is a strong vein of morality running through this story, especially with regard to the seventh commandment, 'Thou shalt not commit adultery'. Are there other occasions when this concern is expressed or implied?

68/70	Rural community

70 The maltster cleared . . .
This description of how long the maltster has lived and the limited area which has been the world he lived in, tends to emphasize the closeness of their world, a world of which Bathsheba and Gabriel are part but in which Boldwood and Troy are really strangers.

69/79	Rural community

71 'She fleed at him, . . .'
With the dismissal of Bailey Pennyways, the author introduces into the reader's mind the possibility of Gabriel stepping into Pennyways' shoes. However, life is never quite so simple and it will be a little while before the opportunity to promote Gabriel is grasped.

68/75	Bathsheba
67/74	Gabriel
53/72	Structure

72 'Fanny Robin—Miss Everdene's . . .'
The long rural interlude with the rustics has now been abruptly interrupted with two major events, both calculated to set the rustics' tongues wagging and the readers guessing. The mysterious girl met at the end of the last chapter is identified, but the reason for her disappearance is yet to be disclosed, and Bathsheba's bailiff has been caught stealing.

60/73	Fanny
71/86	Structure

	Characters and ideas previous/next comment

73 'She had, I think, . . .'
Note the first reference to the soldier, and the prophetic irony of Bathsheba's hope that Fanny comes to no harm through him.

72/77 Fanny

74 That night at Coggan's . . .
How accurate a description do you think is this reference to Gabriel's love for Bathsheba as being like 'a river flowing rapidly under ice'?

71/79 Gabriel

Chapter 9

75 'Maryann, you go!' . . .
Notice how Bathsheba was 'fluttering under the onset of romantic possibilities'. There is no evidence that she was expecting anyone at this time, nor that she had formed any romantic attachments in the short period she had been at Weatherbury. Gabriel was unlikely to ride up to her door, so what set her off must have been her own highly emotional and romantically inclined nature! As irony would have it, why was she perhaps right to 'flutter' at the possibilities?

71/76 Bathsheba

76 A woman's dress . . .
Bathsheba's decision not to receive Mr Boldwood appears to have its origin in the vanity which she displayed when we first made her acquaintance.

75/77 Bathsheba
37/77 Boldwood
61/80 Character

77 'Oh, because, as she . . .'
The discussion that starts about how Mr Boldwood has an interest in Fanny soon turns to a description of how eligible he is and that it would appear most of the young ladies around have broken their hearts over him – without response.

76/78 Bathsheba
73/83 Fanny
76/95 Boldwood

78 'What a pucker . . .'
How aptly could Maryann's comment here about the poor and rich men be applied to Bathsheba?

77/79 Bathsheba

79 'How sweet to be able . . .'
What do you think of Liddy's response when Bathsheba confides that she refused to marry a man because of his lack of social standing? Is it an accurate representation of Bathsheba's true reaction to Gabriel's proposal?

78/80 Bathsheba
74/82 Gabriel
70/80 Rural community
43/98 Love and marriage

Chapter 10

80 The men breathed an . . .
Bathsheba demonstrates unusual independence for a woman of her time. Note how the men were so amazed at her action.

79/81 Bathsheba
76/81 Character
79/84 Rural community

	Characters and ideas *previous*/*next* comment

81 Bathsheba blushed slightly . . .
Contrast this generosity with the previous incident where she argued over a
mere twopence. Has she changed, or is it just that her circumstances have
changed?

80/82	Bathsheba
80/84	Character

82 'Very well then, Cainy . . .'
Was Bathsheba just being deliberately insulting to Gabriel with this remark,
or did she perhaps know of his lost flock and wonder at his competence? Or
is the comment in the next paragraph the key? Certainly she had risen in
social status. Would you agree that she now demonstrates a 'proportionate
increase of arrogance and reserve'? You also ought to consider whether
Bathsheba, being already acquainted with Gabriel and with him being aware
of her humble origins, thought to establish her authority and, as is so often
the case, perhaps overdid it a little.

81/84	Bathsheba
79/107	Gabriel

83 'Yes,' continued William, . . .
What is ironic about the tune the band played as the soldiers left town?

77/87	Fanny
50/98	Fate and irony

84 Then this small thesmothete . . .
Note how Liddy cannot resist the opportunity to imitate Bathsheba's exit
and so draws attention to her slightly vain attitude – no doubt to the
amusement of the rustics.

82/91	Bathsheba
81/89	Character
80/108	Rural community

Chapter 11

85 For dreariness nothing could . . .
Note how we are prepared for events to come when yet again a matter of a
sombre nature is preceded by 'darkness'.

66/86	Nature

86 The changes of the seasons . . .
Read this and the subsequent four paragraphs. Note how the images
presented and the language used build up an oppressive and despairing
atmosphere.

85/87	Nature
72/87	Structure

87 The shape went slowly . . .
Why is it that Fanny is usually pictured alone – an outsider? Note how
darkness and bad weather often surround her. She makes very few
appearances in the novel, but has a profound affect on the lives of which
characters?

83/88	Fanny
86/90	Structure
86/103	Nature

88 'O, Frank – don't you . . .'
What does Fanny mean by calling herself 'Your wife', and what does it
prepare us for?

87/89	Fanny
37/89	Troy

89 'The fact is, I forgot . . .'
Troy is depicted as irresponsible and callous and the reader must feel
pessimistic about the prospects for Fanny's marriage.

84/91	Character
88/112	Fanny
88/112	Troy

90 'Ho – ho – Sergeant . . .'
What is the purpose of this revelation that the conversation has been overheard by a third party? Will the mysterious stranger have something to contribute to the action later in the story? Is the paragraph merely a red herring to create suspense, or is the exclamation a comment on the watcher's opinion of Sergeant Troy's promises – or perhaps all three?

87/103   Structure

Chapter 12

91 Among these heavy . . .
We have already witnessed Bathsheba establishing her position at her own farm, a difficult enough task for an inexperienced girl. But here, at the Corn Exchange amongst experienced farmers, her task is greatly increased. Note how she prepared herself. Being 'prettily and even daintily dressed' was no doubt a help to her own morale, but she required much more than that to establish her credentials among these men.

84/92   Bathsheba
89/93   Character

92 Something in the exact . . .
Note the sensuousness, even outright sexuality of the description of Bathsheba's appearance and manner in this paragraph. It should perhaps prepare us a little for the fairly tempestuous nature of her liaison with Troy. It also has in it something of the sensual nature which underpins the description of Troy's demonstration of his skill with the sword.

91/93   Bathsheba

93 Strange to say of . . .
Note the efficient and effective way with which Bathsheba manages her dealings in the corn market. Would you say that she has altered considerably since we first met her, or were the incidents of the twopence which Gabriel paid and the unexpected bonuses she gave her employees really excellent pointers to a very shrewd business sense?

92/94   Bathsheba
91/94   Character

94 'Yes, 'tis a pity she's . . .'
There is a deal of prophetic irony in this man's assessment of Bathsheba – 'headstrong' and 'she'll soon get picked up'. To what extent would you agree with both these judgments and could you think of incidents which supported them?

93/95   Bathsheba
93/97   Character

95 She soon knew thus . . .
When you consider Bathsheba's first assessment of Boldwood – 'erect in attitude, quiet in demeanour' and pre-eminently dignified, you ought also to wonder what traumas – mental anguish – the man experienced that reduced him to the deranged figure who shot Troy. Does Boldwood finally regain that dignity which Bathsheba so notices now?

94/96   Bathsheba
77/97   Boldwood

96 When marketing was . . .
Do you remember what Gabriel promised to get for Bathsheba when they married? Note that she has not only got the gig, but we will also shortly learn that she has a new piano.

95/97   Bathsheba

	Characters and ideas previous/next comment	

97 'Oh, Farmer Boldwood . . .'
Note the manner of Boldwood's passing. The name William is Germanic in origin and means 'resolute protector'. Do you think Hardy might have had this in mind when he named him, and do you think it apt? Boldwood's aloofness intrigues Bathsheba and she interprets this with a romantic notion.

96/98	Bathsheba
95/100	Boldwood
94/109	Character

Chapter 13

98 The book was open . . .
In the Bible Ruth worked in the fields, ignored the young men and 'lay down' with the farmer who later married her. Should we see any elements of a parallel here with Bathsheba? How does Liddy demonstrate knowledge of the way her mistress's mind is working?

97/99	Bathsheba
83/100	Fate and irony
79/102	Love and marriage

99 Bathsheba paused to regard . . .
Note Bathsheba's thoughts about the fact of Boldwood ignoring her. Do you think that Boldwood is intentionally ignoring her, or does he really have no thought for her at all?

98/101	Bathsheba

100 'He'd worry to death . . .'
A rather ironic statement from Liddy given the actual outcome of Bathsheba sending the valentine card

97/102	Boldwood
98/101	Fate and irony

101 Bathsheba, a small yawn . . .
Does this 'small yawn' say more about Bathsheba's mental attitude than she intends?

99/102	Bathsheba
100/102	Fate and irony

102 So very idly and . . .
What incident can you think of to support the view that Bathsheba had a fair knowledge of love 'as a spectacle'? Would it be fair to suggest she viewed Gabriel's courtship as a 'spectacle'? 'Idly and unreflectingly was this deed done' – from this point in the novel, Bathsheba will begin to suffer the repercussions of her thoughtless action.

101/105	Bathsheba
101/103	Fate and irony
100/103	Boldwood
98/103	Love and marriage

Chapter 14

103 At dusk on the evening . . .
Note the evening setting, always a time for threatening events. What is prophetically ironic about the red seal becoming as 'a blot of blood' in Boldwood's eye? Why should the reader be surprised by Boldwood's reaction to this letter?

87/106	Nature
90/107	Structure
102/104	Boldwood
102/104	Fate and irony

	Characters and ideas previous/next comment

104 Since the receipt of the . . .
Note how massively the arrival of the valentine has affected Boldwood. Certainly his reaction ought to prepare us for the traumatic events to follow.

103/105 Boldwood
103/116 Fate and irony

105 The solemn and reserved . . .
There is an interesting parallel here. We see again a concern with looking at one's reflection in a mirror, but one could hardly accuse Boldwood of vanity – or could one?

102/109 Bathsheba
104/106 Boldwood

106 It was one of . . .
Notice the imagery – sunrise that resembled sunset over Weatherbury Upper Farm. The sunrise that should have suggested hope for Boldwood, only serves to emphasize his disorientation after receiving the valentine.

105/107 Boldwood
103/124 Nature

107 'I don't think it . . .'
Notice how Hardy moves the novel's action forward by the misdirection of the letter, enabling Boldwood and Gabriel to meet, and the lives of Fanny and the four main characters to become inextricably entwined.

106/113 Boldwood
82/110 Gabriel
103/108 Structure

Chapter 15

108 The maltster, after having . . .
This is another of those long conversations between the rustics, providing us with an insight into their lives. It also causes suspense as the reader waits for Boldwood and Gabriel to meet so that the contents of the letter may be discovered, and so move the plot forward.

84/129 Rural community
107/114 Structure

109 'A headstrong maid, . . .'
To what extent would you accept this view that Bathsheba's problems stem from a mixture of pride and vanity, and presumably her headstrong nature?

105/117 Bathsheba
97/111 Character

110 'Mark,' said Gabriel . . .
The simple and open honesty of Gabriel's love for Bathsheba comes across here. Contrast it with the ways of Troy and Boldwood later in the novel.

107/111 Gabriel

111 'I don't mind owning . . .'
Gabriel seems to have accepted that his position is hopeless, and not just for the post of bailiff. But is there a symbolically hopeful note in the revival of the near lifeless young lambs which are mentioned in the next paragraph?

109/114 Character
110/112 Gabriel

112 'DEAR FRIEND – I do . . .'
Fanny's letter shows her simplicity and trust in both Gabriel and Troy – a trust which is to be broken on both counts, by Gabriel immediately, when he shows the letter to Boldwood, and by Troy later.

111/114 Gabriel
89/115 Fanny
89/115 Troy

113 'Fanny – poor Fanny! . . .'
Boldwood's concern for Fanny's future is based on knowledge of Troy. Consider the irony in his concern for Fanny's fate at the hands of Troy.

107/114 Boldwood

114 Oak had coloured . . .
Coming hard on the heels of the rustics' comments about how he was 'hard done' by Bathsheba, the realization of what Boldwood's question might mean comes as a blow for Gabriel. Note however, that it is Boldwood who finds the news 'torture'.

Chapter 16

115 The silence grew . . .
Notice how the whole of this scene is effectively written against the background of the seemingly leering clock; it is an image which builds up the tension, the 'leer' suggesting that all will not go well.

116 'Ah, when? God . . .
Troy's words, spoken with some bitterness are more prophetic than he could realize. What does the incident tell us of his character? It is obvious from later events that he does love Fanny. It is strange, then, that he treats her in this way. Is his pride and vanity so cruelly taxed at this point that he is incapable of doing the right thing now – only to bitterly regret it later? He appears to have something in common with Bathsheba here.

Chapter 17

117 On Saturday Boldwood . . .
The allusion to Adam's first sight of Eve stresses the growth of Boldwood's obsession and warns of impending disaster – remember what happened to Adam's Garden of Eden after he had fallen prey to Eve's temptations.

118 Boldwood looked at her . . .
There is a tremendous contrast in these next two paragraphs between the way Boldwood 'dimly understood' women, and the way he looked at Bathsheba. The evidence for the deep trauma that Boldwood was going through as a result of Bathsheba's thoughtlessness is plain to see.

119 And this charming woman . . .
Note how well this paragraph foreshadows coming events. 'Boldwood's blindness' and 'Bathsheba's insensibility' to the results of 'little beginnings' are the source of much of the tragedy that will follow.

120 All this time . . .
Note the images of 'artificial flower' and 'wax fruit' which reinforce the insincerity behind Bathsheba's action.

121 She that day nearly . . .
Bathsheba recognizes, too late, the quandry she has placed herself in. It also leaves the reader in some suspense, wondering how she will manage to resolve the problem she has created.

Chapter 18

122 Pacing up and down . . .
As with other characters, the author here gives us an insight into Boldwood
and the inner workings of his mind. Note those words which give some clue
to the origin of his present state: cloister, celibate, meditate, stillness, stern,
serious, and contrast them with those perceptions he had of Bathsheba in
the previous chapter. This is not a man to ignore such a valentine as
Bathsheba had sent him.

123 The phases of Boldwood's . . .
In this description of Boldwood, Hardy presents us with a clearly drawn
picture of a man whose emotional balance is extremely fine. The fine
adjustment of his positive and negative qualities has been disturbed and the
consequences are about to unfold.

124 It was now early spring–. . .
The natural world moves inexorably on, and those human passions bred
during the winter will start their growth. Note how a few paragraphs on
Boldwood is described as 'now living outside his defences'.

125 He approached the gate . . .
This pastoral scene where Gabriel and Bathsheba work together with the
sheep has a feeling of peace and rightness, which even the approach of the
tormented Boldwood cannot quite destroy. Be aware of other scenes where a
similar picture is presented.

126 At once connecting . . .
Is Gabriel justified in putting down this approach of Boldwood just to a
'coquettish procedure' on Bathsheba's part? Is there any way in which she
can be entirely blamed for the state that Boldwood is in?

127 As for Bathsheba . . .
We are given a clear insight here into Bathsheba's reaction to the flame she
has kindled. She is not a flirt and a schemer, and instantly resolves never to
do anything so thoughtless again. Ironically however, the resolve is too late,
and her earlier worries that whatever she said to Boldwood would be
misinterpreted are tragically confirmed here.

Chapter 19

128 Boldwood did eventually . . .
The great rhythms of nature are emphasized here in the way they act to foil
Boldwood's intention to speak to Bathsheba. Boldwood, despite the fact that
he is a farmer, has forgotten the pressures that nature imposes on the
farming community. It is a measure of how far his own mental balance has
been disturbed.

129 The sheep-washing pool . . .
The description of the sheep-washing pool 'full of the clearest water', the
light sky, the swelling reeds and the 'new, soft, and moist' leaves combine to
create yet another of those natural scenes which serve to balance the action
of this story.

	Characters and ideas previous/next comment

130 'I feel – almost too . . .'
Look back to chapter 4, when Gabriel proposed marriage to Bathsheba. In some ways these two men are very similar, just as determined and intense as each other, but their reactions to situations and events are very different.

127/131	Bathsheba
123/132	Boldwood
102/133	Love and marriage

131 'I – I didn't – I . . .'
The decision that Bathsheba found so difficult to make is now forced upon her. As events have turned out, would it have been better if she had approached Boldwood first in an attempt to put his mind at rest and before he had time to dwell on the incident and its possible implications? Certainly, she is now forced to face the consequences of her vanity and irresponsibility.

130/133	Bathsheba

132 'But you will just . . .'
It is interesting to compare the things that Boldwood offered to Bathsheba with those offered by Gabriel. Both proposals tell us something about the two men, and the things they assume the woman in their life will want. Which was possibly the most carefully judged list of 'gifts' – given the respective state of knowledge that the two men had of Bathsheba?

130/133	Boldwood
126/137	Gabriel

133 Bathsheba's heart was . . .
Bathsheba's honest rejection of Boldwood's proposal is tempered by remorse and pity. Is her 'pride and vanity' more than just the inexperience of youth?

131/134	Bathsheba
132/134	Boldwood
130/134	Love and marriage

134 'Say then, that . . .'
How does Boldwood manage to retain some hope that Bathsheba might accept him? Given your knowledge of the man how do you think he would have reacted to a more brutal rejection on Bathsheba's part? Perhaps it would have been 'kinder, to be cruel'.

133/136	Bathsheba
133/135	Boldwood
133/140	Love and marriage

Chapter 20

135 Yet Farmer Boldwood . . .
Note this comment on Boldwood's proposal of marriage. In his unbalanced state is he thinking much more of himself and his own happiness than of Bathsheba?

134/140	Boldwood

136 Bathsheba, not being . . .
This exploration of the motives behind two parties wanting to marry is interesting. It certainly highlights the peculiar position – in most people's view – in which Bathsheba found herself. She was an independent woman ruling in a man's world. Her position 'was a novel one' and she was determined to exploit it and enjoy it to the full.

134/138	Bathsheba
129/147	Rural community

137 The next day to . . .
This image of peace and war grimly foreshadows the events which will shortly take place.

132/138	Gabriel

	Characters and ideas	
	previous/next comment	

138 He relinquished the . . .
We frequently see Gabriel and Bathsheba united in work; this though is their first physical contact – shortly to end in a quarrel!

136/139	Bathsheba
137/139	Gabriel

139 'Did the men think . . .'
What are Bathsheba's reasons for asking Gabriel about what the men thought of her meeting with Boldwood? Is she concerned about a possible scandal and loss of dignity? Or could she, subconsciously or otherwise, be interested in finding out Gabriel's reaction?

138/140	Bathsheba
138/140	Gabriel

140 'Miss Everdene, you . . .'
Notice how Bathsheba's insistence on the use of her surname contrasts with the intimate nature of their conversation. Is this a not very successful attempt to maintain her dignity?

135/158	Boldwood
139/141	Bathsheba
139/141	Gabriel
134/141	Love and marriage

141 'Well, what is your . . .'
Despite her perplexity with Gabriel, she ploughs on regardless and asks for his opinion of her conduct. Gabriel seems to be bereft of tact, but perhaps he feels that unlike Bathsheba's response to Boldwood, an honest question requires an honest answer. But having given the answer, he must then rub salt in her wounds. Gabriel too, has a lot to learn about how to cope with the feelings of other people.

140/142	Bathsheba
123/145	Character
114/196	Gabriel
140/143	Love and marriage

142 A woman may be treated . . .
This analysis of Bathsheba's reaction to Gabriel's words and attitude shows her at her most vulnerable. She has yet to attain that maturity which would enable her to deal with the situation without losing control of it, or her temper.

141/143	Bathsheba

143 'Go at once then . . .'
What for both Gabriel and Bathsheba must at times have been an unsatisfactory and sometimes embarrassing relationship is ended when they both re-establish their independence – but for how long?

142/145	Bathsheba
141/148	Gabriel
141/154	Love and marriage

Chapter 21

144 Gabriel Oak had ceased . . .
The narrative is tied very closely to the rhythms of nature and the activities of the farmer. At some stage in the story Gabriel and Bathsheba will need to re-establish relationships, with both of them having to come to terms with the fact that their relationship has undergone a quite substantial change as a result of the outspoken disagreement on the matter of Bathsheba's conduct with Boldwood. This incident of the sheep's illness may seem to have come a bit soon after their argument, but in terms of agricultural reality it is a quite feasible happening – and at the right time of the year.

121/146	Structure

145 Her eyes were at . . .
Note the reference to the 'dashing velvet dress, carefully put on before a glass'. Bathsheba may have received an object lesson in the foolishness of her unthinking ways, but not sufficiently to dent her vanity!

143/147   Bathsheba
141/164   Character

146 Many of them foamed . . .
You will recall that it was the destruction of Gabriel's flock shortly after Bathsheba had rejected his proposal of marriage that made him glad he had no wife, drove him away from his farm and into Weatherbury where Bathsheba was farming. Now, it is the threat to her flock, again shortly after she had 'rejected' his services, that bring them together again. Their lives are tied to the land. It is worth noting that Farmer Boldwood eventually takes to neglecting his farm, as indeed does Troy once he has married Bathsheba. There is no such neglect on either Gabriel's or Bathsheba's part.

144/151   Structure

147 'Shepherd Oak,' said . . .
The country worker's respect for Gabriel's skills as a shepherd help to reinforce the suspense of the moment, providing yet another quandry for Bathsheba to solve. However, she has to make a clear-cut choice between the death of her sheep and a blow to her vanity, a much clearer choice than she has had before but not one that could be put off for a moment.

145/149   Bathsheba
136/156   Rural
           community

148 'He says *beggars mustn't* . . . .
This is hardly a reply calculated to please Bathsheba! However, it must be viewed in the light of her first message, itself rude and thoughtless. But Gabriel's full reply, 'as becomes any 'ooman . . .' repeats quite forcefully the import of what he had said to Bathsheba when she asked his opinion of her conduct with Boldwood, and emphasizes the essential honesty of the man. He is not prepared to allow the rustics to indulge in any scurrilous gossip about Bathsheba, but he will not hesitate to comment in both private and public when she is quite evidently doing wrong.

143/151   Gabriel

149 'Oh, oh, that's his . . .'
This is perhaps the crux of the matter for Bathsheba's vanity with regard to Gabriel. There is something quite pointed and humorous in the way another of the flock, as if in reply 'sprang into the air, and fell dead' – a fairly forceful argument which puts 'airs' and the question of who shall 'beg' into the correct perspective.

147/150   Bathsheba

150 'I wouldn't cry . . .'
Bathsheba is quick to take up the proffered advice of the rustic; it is after all very sound.

149/151   Bathsheba

151 After this collapse . . .
Why does Bathsheba feel moved to add the message 'Do not desert me, Gabriel!'? It has an echo about it of the message attached to the valentine – 'Marry me', but does it have the same effect on its reader?

150/153   Bathsheba
148/152   Gabriel
146/153   Structure

152 Gabriel was already . . .
Notice the realism of the sheep's illness and the cure compared with the element of fate where Gabriel is the only man able to cure the illness.

116/163   Fate and
           irony
151/153   Gabriel
147/155   Rural
           community

153 It has been said . . .
Gabriel's skills and enduring character overcome this natural disaster and help save Bathsheba's flock. Note how he helps her on two other occasions when he saves her ricks from fire in chapter 6, and the storm in chapter 37. Each time the events mark a new stage in their relationship.

152/154	Gabriel
151/165	Structure
151/154	Bathsheba

154 When the love-led . . .
Bathsheba would seem to know quite well that she can manipulate Gabriel to do her will if she uses her femininity, but equally she will be aware that there are quite strict limitations on the nature of what she can make him do. In this respect he is still very much his 'own man'. The scene is set for Gabriel's advancement.

143/155	Love and marriage
153/157	Bathsheba
153/157	Gabriel

Chapter 22

155 It was the first day . . .
Another of the year's great occasions was the sheep-shearing. The image of nature, plump with promise of good things to harvest with its 'racing currents of juice', is a fitting time for the forwarding of romantic relationships between Bathsheba and the two competitors for her hand, Boldwood and Gabriel.

154/157	Love and marriage
152/156	Rural community
129/156	Nature

156 They sheared in the . . .
There is a sense of timelessness evoked in this description of the great barn; similar in form to the neighbouring church and vying with it for antiquity, its use for shearing, also an age-old practice, echoes the continuity and harmony of man and nature. Do read the description carefully, looking for all those other references to history, religion and man which the author so vividly draws.

155/157	Nature
155/160	Rural community

157 Bathsheba, after throwing . . .
Notice the delicate sensuality of this scene between Bathsheba and Gabriel. The two of them, separate from the other shearers, are as in a world of their own. Study the language used to describe the scene and be aware of how the author conveys the atmosphere of intimacy by such words and phrases as 'lopped off . . . and collar', 'quietly looking on', 'insult', 'murmured', 'pink flush' etc. Note Gabriel's reaction, happy to be alone with Bathsheba with a silence that 'says much'.

155/166	Love and marriage
156/165	Nature
154/166	Bathsheba
154/166	Gabriel

158 But heartless circumstance . . .
Boldwood's appearance disrupts the happy, sensuous mood in the barn. From 'Aphrodite' we are suddenly pitched into the harsh realities of 'rams and old ewes', 'shearlings and hogs'.

157/159	Bathsheba
157/161	Gabriel
140/162	Boldwood

159 'O Gabriel!' she . . .
What persuades Bathsheba to criticize Gabriel in this way, especially as she must know she is partly responsible for the wound? Is it that the sudden appearance of Boldwood has unsettled her and she is venting her resulting displeasure on Gabriel—as a scapegoat for her own guilty feelings?

158/163	Bathsheba

		Characters and ideas previous/next comment

160 'That means matrimony,' . . .
The author again uses the rustics to comment on the immediate action, at the same time giving us over the next few pages yet another insight into their lives and attitudes.

156/161 Rural community

---

161 'What a lie!' said . . .
Yet again Gabriel defends Bathsheba's reputation against the rustics' gossip. Note however, how shortly Gabriel will ruminate on what he considers to be the misjustice he is being done. It is interesting to compare these moments of introspection with the way Boldwood reacts to the unpredictable Bathsheba.

158/162 Gabriel
160/218 Rural community

Chapter 23

162 At this moment . . .
Bathsheba knew that Boldwood would be coming to the supper yet she asked Gabriel to take a place which must surely have been meant for Boldwood. Certainly there is no way in which another farmer would have expected to sit with the hired help. In making Gabriel yield the place of honour at table she certainly 'puts him in his place', but does she thereby also elevate Boldwood to a position any more than his status as gentleman-farmer would in any case demand?

158/197 Boldwood
161/192 Gabriel

---

163 She stood up in the . . .
What is prophetically ironic about the words of Bathsheba's song? The 'rich unexplored shadow' which their group comprised is surely symbolic of the problems and tribulations which are about to beset them.

159/164 Bathsheba
152/169 Fate and irony

---

164 'I have every reason . . .'
What is it that has brought Bathsheba to the point of saying yes to Boldwood's proposal? Certainly there is a grim irony in her use of the phrase 'between this time and harvest' which doesn't bode well for the promise. Is she just in love with the idea of being in love, it being more of an adventure than a real commitment? The situation was not 'without its fearful joy' for her, so is it her vanity alone that has driven her to make this agreement with Boldwood?

163/166 Bathsheba
145/167 Character

Chapter 24

165 Among the multifarious . . .
It is again dark, and Bathsheba, in the midst of that darkness will have her first encounter with Troy. The tension is built up by an emphasis on Bathsheba's freedom from any suspicion that what she is doing might be dangerous. As before, however, when danger or turmoil is present the author's descriptions tend to eventually concentrate on those aspects of the natural world which add to the oppressive atmosphere. Note how three paragraphs on he describes the scene, talking of the night as 'black as the ninth plague' and mentioning such things as 'dead spikelets' and 'mildewed cones'.

157/181 Nature
153/170 Structure

---

166 'We have got hitched . . .'
Would you agree that beginning with this phrase there is a deal of imagery

164/167 Bathsheba

in their conversation and actions which could reasonably have double meanings: 'Are you a woman? . . . I am a man', and so on?

116/167	Troy
157/182	Love and marriage

167 He looked hard into . . .
Read the detail of their encounter carefully. To what extent does Troy make a quite distinct appeal to Bathsheba's vanity, and what is her response?

166/168	Bathsheba
164/173	Character
166/169	Troy

168 'I deserve the . . .'
How would you describe Bathsheba's attitude to 'her father's sex'? Troy was of course referring to all men, but it is interesting to remember how the rustics describe Mr Everdene's view of his wife and how Troy, once married to Bathsheba, suddenly seems to find other matters more interesting—a curious reversal of the situation Troy had in mind!

167/169	Bathsheba

169 'What, Beauty, and drag . . .'
There is a certain irony in Troy's words here. It certainly seems to be the case that both Fanny and Bathsheba find themselves traipsing around the countryside in pursuit of Sergeant Troy!

168/170	Bathsheba
163/182	Fate and irony
167/170	Troy

170 'No, stranger. Sergeant Troy . . .'
It is interesting how the three men in Bathsheba's life no sooner get into conversation with her than their thoughts seem to turn to marriage. Look back at her conversations with Boldwood and Gabriel to see when they first made direct or oblique references to marriage.

165/172	Structure
169/171	Bathsheba
169/171	Troy

171 After all, how could . . .
How has Liddy's account of Troy's background affected Bathsheba's feelings about him? Did Gabriel or Boldwood ever attempt to praise or 'master' Bathsheba?

170/176	Bathsheba
170/172	Troy

Chapter 25

172 Idiosyncrasy and vicissitude . . .
As he has done with the other main characters, the author here sketches Troy's character is some detail, but much more so than any of the others. Does his character need more explanation because of the way in which he will destroy Fanny and Boldwood, cause a great deal of grief and pain to Gabriel and come close to ruining Bathsheba?

171/173	Troy
170/179	Structure

173 He was a man to . . .
Is the phrase 'a man to whom memories were an incumbrance, and anticipation a superfluity', the import of which is largely rephrased and repeated a few lines on, really completely fair to Troy? He certainly has remorse over his treatment of Fanny. To a certain extent, does Bathsheba deserve to suffer for the vanity which led her to marry Sergeant Troy, despite her promise to Boldwood and the undying devotion of Gabriel?

172/174	Troy
167/174	Character

Characters and ideas previous/next comment

174 The wondrous power . . .
Read this paragraph on flattery. Do you think that Troy 'acquires powers reaching to the extremity of perdition'? Certainly, in Bathsheba he has perhaps found the right person on whom to try his powers of flattery.

173/176	Character
173/175	Troy

175 He had been known . . .
Who treats other people fairly? Is Boldwood's treatment of Bathsheba fair or is he more concerned with his own feelings? Consider whether Gabriel disproves Troy's contention – 'Treat them fairly, and you are a lost man'.

174/177	Troy

Chapter 26

176 'Don't – don't! I . . .'
Notice Bathsheba's confusion in the face of Troy's flattering barrage of words. She seems to be faced with some painful choices and is torn between establishing her social position, her role as an independent woman and her desire to hear more.

171/177	Bathsheba
174/196	Character

177 'O, it is true enough . . .'
Troy makes an interesting comment on Bathsheba's beauty and its effect on men. To what extent do you think there is some truth in his remarks – with regard to the three main male characters of this story?

176/178	Bathsheba
175/179	Troy

178 'Well, you need not . . .'
On which other occasions has Bathsheba shown a concern about people speaking their minds to her? It certainly seems that she is wary of being told 'home truths'. It could be because subconsciously she is aware of her faults but realizes she is not yet in control of them.

177/179	Bathsheba

179 And before she knew . . .
The gift of the watch symbolizes the extravagant moment, a turning point in both lives. Note the startling effect it has on Bathsheba. Is it just Troy's flattery, playing on Bathsheba's vanity which brings such a strong response from her?

178/180	Bathsheba
172/184	Structure
177/181	Troy

180 Bathsheba could not face . . .
Bathsheba is perhaps more flustered here than she has been at any time with either Gabriel or Boldwood. If she could have tried a little harder to find the answer to her own question – how much of it is true – she might have discovered the truth, but is the key to her state of mind that really she did not want to know the answer?

179/181	Bathsheba

Chapter 27

181 The Weatherbury bees . . .
The season – mid-summer – matches the development of the action. Bathsheba and Troy's love will be as intense and short-lived as the summer heat. It is perhaps fitting that bees, which flit from one flower to another in gathering their honey, should form the setting for Bathsheba's next encounter with Troy.

180/182	Bathsheba
165/201	Nature
179/182	Troy

182 'But you must have on . . .'
'Whimsical fate' dictates that Bathsheba should again be in close physical contact with Troy as she dresses him in protective clothing. There is an echo here of the scene when Bathsheba and Troy first met.

169/206	Fate and irony
181/183	Bathsheba
181/183	Troy
166/186	Love and marriage

183 An unconscious look of . . .
Why would they both feel that Liddy would be 'superfluous'? Is it that they both sense their meeting will be rather climactic in their relationship?

182/185	Troy
182/186	Bathsheba

Chapter 28

184 At eight o'clock . . .
The association of different times of the day with dramatic events is continued here with Bathsheba and Troy meeting in the evening, but for what? Is it just a sword display?

179/185	Structure

185 She saw a dim spot . . .
Is the author providing a structural link here with the reference to the spot of 'red'; a 'spot' which will shortly loom very large in Bathsheba's life? Boldwood too, saw a spot of red that became ever larger and inflamed in his eyes. Do you remember what it was? Is there a parallel here in the way Boldwood reacted to Bathsheba with the way she reacts to Troy? Certainly, at the end of the story some of the symbolism which surrounds the colour red will find its fulfilment in the death of Troy at Boldwood's hand.

184/189	Structure
183/186	Troy

186 'Now,' said Troy . . .
Troy's sword is 'like a living thing'. As we shall see, the dazzling display of skill will not only symbolize Troy's ability to dominate a woman, but also actually lead to the eventual capitulation of Bathsheba. Note those words and phrases which emphasize the sensuousness of this scene, though do be wary of reading too much into every word.

185/187	Troy
183/187	Bathsheba
182/187	Love and marriage

187 In an instant the . . .
Notice the use of the light image in connection with Troy's masterful performance. Bathsheba is dazzled physically, emotionally and sexually.

186/188	Bathsheba
186/188	Love and marriage
186/193	Troy

188 Bathsheba, overcome by . . .
Bathsheba, 'overcome by a hundred tumultuous feelings' resulting from the scene with the sword, is left 'powerless to withstand or deny him'. This is a turning point in their relationship and you might like to consider how, if at all, Bathsheba's behaviour has any parallel with that of Boldwood – a person also out of his senses with 'love'.

187/189	Bathsheba
187/194	Love and marriage

189 She saw him stoop . . .
Remember this act of Troy's. Later in the novel you will notice that Troy has in his possession a lock of hair, but it is not Bathsheba's and it becomes the key to Troy's undoing.

188/190	Bathsheba
115/223	Fanny
185/201	Structure

Chapter 29

190 We now see the . . .
Our comment made earlier that perhaps Bathsheba did not want to know
Troy's true character, is commented on more fully here by the author. Take
note of this fairly detailed consideration that the author gives of Bathsheba's
motives and character here and in the following paragraphs.

189/191   Bathsheba

191 'Since this subject has . . .'
How accurate is Bathsheba's account of her agreement with Boldwood? She
felt obliged to give Gabriel an account of her actions once before; can you
recall when and in what circumstances?

190/192   Bathsheba

192 'I say–I say again–. . .'
Note the irony in Bathsheba's praise of Troy for being blunt 'sometimes even
to rudeness'. This is the very reason for which she actually dismissed Gabriel
at one time.

191/193   Bathsheba
163/194   Gabriel

193 'The reason of that . . .'
If Bathsheba had wanted to she could have discovered the falsity of Troy's
claim herself. He does not seem to be the sort of man who would humbly
creep in by the back way to church. Do you think he really would have
struck Bathsheba in that way, if she had bothered to think about it?

192/194   Bathsheba
187/194   Troy

194 'You know, mistress, . . .'
Study Gabriel's reaction to Bathsheba's relationship with Troy. How does he
demonstrate his strength of character here?

193/197   Bathsheba
192/195   Gabriel
188/198   Love and
          marriage
193/207   Troy

195 'That's nonsense,' said Oak . . .
As he rightly comments this is not the first time Bathsheba has told him to
go. Gabriel acts with some dignity and not a little annoyance. He is a touch
more masterful in his relationship with Bathsheba here than at any time
previously. Perhaps he is beginning to tire of being so placid and self-
effacing.

194/196   Gabriel

196 Gabriel went home . . .
Gabriel discovers the truth about Troy's churchgoing habits. How, in the
eyes of the reader, does Gabriel emerge from the events of this chapter? Has
he changed in any way from the man we first met in chapter 1?

176/198   Character
195/212   Gabriel

Chapter 30

197 In three minutes . . .
Bathsheba at last stops putting off decisions and finds herself compelled to
write immediately to Boldwood, putting an end to their relationship and his

194/198   Bathsheba
162/203   Boldwood

hopes of marriage. Why does she feel it so important to do this, and with such a rush to get it posted? If it is an act of desperation, of what is she frightened?

198 'Who are you speaking of?' . . .
Notice how the author indicates Bathsheba's confused state of mind as she manipulates the conversation with her women – making contradictory statements and looking for reassurance.

197/199	Bathsheba
196/202	Character
194/200	Love and marriage

199 'No, no Liddy; . . .'
Note the irony of Bathsheba suggesting she will die in the workhouse. Who does die there?

198/200	Bathsheba

200 'I don't often cry . . .'
It is some measure of the desperate circumstances in which Bathsheba finds herself that she seems determined to believe Troy really is all she wants him to be, even to the extent of asking Liddy to support her in the lie.

199/204	Bathsheba
198/215	Love and marriage

Chapter 31

201 The next evening . . .
It is evening again, and the scene is set for the storm about to break around Bathsheba's head. Note the ominous imagery in the next paragraph of 'lairs of fierce light' which were before her in the sky as she left the house on her journey.

181/217	Nature
189/202	Structure

202 Boldwood had for the . . .
The 'sorry gleams from a broken mirror' remind us of those many times when Bathsheba studied her appearance in a mirror, and of how Boldwood kept her valentine tucked into the corner of his mirror, a mirror which in his turn he studied himself.

198/203	Character
201/208	Structure

203 Bathsheba commanded herself . . .
Is it only now that Bathsheba, and the reader, can really appreciate the full extent to which Boldwood's character is flawed?

197/204	Boldwood
202/230	Character

204 'But there was a time . . .'
Be aware of the balance in the conversation between Bathsheba and Boldwood. Note his long speeches, many of them well reasoned and not without justification in their accusations. In contrast, Bathsheba's replies are very brief. She clearly is not in control of the situation.

200/205	Bathsheba
203/206	Boldwood

205 She checked emotion, . . .
We get the impression from her quiet, clear look that she is attempting to be honest with Boldwood. What do you think of her answer? Note the ominously prophetic remark she makes about what was 'death' to Boldwood.

204/207	Bathsheba

206 'I know you cannot . . .'
It is ironic that Boldwood should accuse the man Bathsheba loves of stealing from him the very things that Bathsheba has so often demonstrated that she lays great store by – respect, good name and standing.

204/208	Boldwood
182/210	Fate and irony

207 'Then curse him . . .'
Note the prophetic nature of Boldwood's curse, but perhaps more importantly note Bathsheba's reaction to the curse. Her every thought is for Troy.

205/208	Bathsheba
194/208	Troy

208 She felt wretchedly . . .
Boldwood's threat to take revenge on Troy creates a new element of suspense to keep the reader's interest. It will eventually lead to the destruction of both of them.

207/209	Bathsheba
206/212	Boldwood
202/211	Structure
207/212	Troy

209 With almost a morbid . . .
Again nature mirrors man: the position Bathsheba finds herself in, 'this guideless woman', finds a reflection in the 'indecisive and palpitating stars'. There is a hint of things to come when we are told that 'Her troubled spirit was far away with Troy'. Soon she will be with him in more than spirit.

208/212	Bathsheba

Chapter 32

210 The village of Weatherbury . . .
Why has this image of the village being like a graveyard a certain irony to it?

206/212	Fate and irony

211 Two varieties only of . . .
The conclusion that the 'thief' is not a woman creates a deal of uncertainty in our minds. The introduction of thieves in the shape of gipsies would be a rather sizeable 'red herring' to draw across the reader's trail at this moment as there is enough happening without this. We are left then, with trying to guess which of the main characters is involved, with very little evidence to point at any of them.

208/213	Structure

212 'Mr Boldwood's Tidy and . . .'
There is a certain irony involved in borrowing Boldwood's horses to chase the 'thief' – which will be appreciated once the thief's identity is revealed. Do you think the chase smacks a little of the melodramatic, with Coggan 'reading the trail' like some sharp-eyed Indian?

209/214	Bathsheba
210/218	Fate and irony
196/220	Gabriel
208/214	Boldwood
208/216	Troy

213 Gabriel looked at . . .
Notice how Hardy uses a similar technique to that in chapter 6, when he also hid Bathsheba's identity until the chapter's climax.

211/217	Structure

214 'True,' she said . . .
More than any of them, Bathsheba can see the irony and embarrassment of their having borrowed Boldwood's horses to chase after her.

212/215	Bathsheba
212/222	Boldwood

215 Bathsheba's perturbed meditations . . .

Bathsheba can see quite clearly what a relationship with Troy will bring her. However, her determination to be rid of him is undermined by her infatuation–or do you think it could be love? Certainly, as the author suggests, a meeting is one way of being sure of seeing him again, and after that–who knows? Perhaps Bathsheba, at the back of her mind, wants to be swept away from the sensible course and allowed to satisfy the passion that she has for this man–regardless of the consequences.

214/216	Bathsheba
200/216	Love and marriage

216 But could she go . . .

Has Bathsheba been a creature of fate in the past, allowing things to take their course and worrying about the consequences later? Certainly, here she indicates she would rather anything happen than that. Yet, in this visit to Troy is she not being swept along by emotions and events, which will 'take their course' almost regardless of her wishes? Note also that her resolution is only a negative one; she will give up Troy and tell him so–not that she will marry Boldwood or Gabriel. If she had decided to take a positive action she might have found herself in a very different situation.

215/225	Bathsheba
215/222	Love and marriage
212/222	Troy

Chapter 33

217 Another week passed . . .

The heat and oppressiveness, the 'monochromatic' sky and trembling air combine to create a fittingly unsettled atmosphere at the farm–in preparation for the story which is about to unfold.

201/219	Nature
213/221	Structure

218 'I hope nothing is . . .'

Another long conversation takes place between the rustics which tells us a great deal about their lives and the times, at the same time as keeping the reader, and Gabriel, in suspense as Cain slowly and painfully retells what he saw in Bath. Notice how the broken key, a recognized omen of bad luck, acts as an appropriate introduction to Cain's story, a story that has much to amuse the reader in the telling of it.

212/258	Fate and irony
161/219	Rural community

219 'He's been dressed up . . .'

See how closely the life of countryfolk is tied to the demands of nature: Cain has a holiday because he is ill, Poorgrass's bad leg allowed him to read *Pilgrim's Progress*, card games and even courting are all done under the excuse of real or imagined illness.

217/226	Nature
218/234	Rural community

220 Then the reapers' hooks . . .

Gabriel's hopes would seem to have been totally dashed by this news. However, do you think he really takes the attitude that it does not matter whose sweetheart Bathsheba is, if she can't be his?

212/227	Gabriel

Chapter 34

221 That same evening . . .

It is again evening, and by this time we should be well prepared for the fact that the events to come will be of a traumatic nature for one or more of the characters.

217/225	Structure

	Characters and ideas
	previous/next comment

222 Troy turned up the . . .
This confrontation between Troy and Boldwood clearly demonstrates the nearly deranged nature of Boldwood. It was suggested earlier that his 'love' of Bathsheba was perhaps more to do with the satisfaction of his own desires than any really deep and abiding love for Bathsheba. However, what does his reaction to the news of Troy's marriage suggest? The other matter that comes across very clearly is Troy's character. The controlled cynicism that he demonstrated in the sword scene finds its fruition here in the way he taunts and 'plays' with Boldwood. The indifference to the suffering of others that was suggested in his dealings with Fanny finds a cruel fulfilment in his treatment of Boldwood.

214/224	Boldwood
216/223	Love and marriage
216/223	Troy

223 'I like Fanny best,' . . .
What is ominous about Troy's statement? Note how he goes on to replace 'like' with 'love' a few lines down. To what extent does he accurately assess the situation when he comments that 'Miss Everdene inflamed me, and displaced Fanny for a time'?

189/250	Fanny
222/246	Love and marriage
222/224	Troy

224 Boldwood loosened his hand . . .
Boldwood's words, 'I've a mind to kill you', foreshadow and prepare us for events later in the novel.

223/228	Boldwood
222/228	Troy

225 Troy handed a folded . . .
Who first promised Bathsheba that their marriage would be announced in a newspaper? Which of the other substantial promises that were made at that time have been fulfilled or are yet to be so? Did any of them come from the person who offered them and is this perhaps a clue as to why they are 'turning to dust'?

216/227	Bathsheba
221/231	Structure

Chapter 35

226 It was very early . . .
What does the language of this passage, the 'confused beginnings', the 'wan blue', the 'thin webs', 'creeping plants . . . bowed' suggest to the observant reader?

219/229	Nature

227 'I fancied we should . . .'
Gabriel's reaction to the fact that Bathsheba and Troy are obviously now married gives us some indication of the depth of his feelings. Contrast his reaction with that of Boldwood.

225/232	Bathsheba
220/228	Gabriel

228 Gabriel soon decided . . .
Do both Gabriel and Boldwood reach the same conclusion about the best way to react to Bathsheba's marriage – and for the same reasons?

224/230	Boldwood
227/233	Gabriel
224/229	Troy

229 'Yes – I suppose so; . . .'
Troy's first thoughts would appear to be about changing the appearance of the farmhouse. He is not a true man of the country in the sense that Bathsheba, Gabriel and the rustics are. His ways are foreign to their lives, out of tune with nature and will shortly lead to near disaster for Bathsheba, the farm and the rustics.

226/232	Nature
228/231	Troy

	Characters and ideas previous/next comment	

230 'Oh Coggan,' said Troy, . . .
Read to the end of the chapter and look for those indications of Hardy warning the reader of Boldwood's eventual behaviour.

228/245	Boldwood
203/237	Character

231 Troy threw the coin . . .
Troy has now thrown money at both of his competitor's for Bathsheba's hand. What does his action say of his character? The contempt with which he treats these two men foreshadows the manner with which he will treat his responsibilities as husband and employer.

225/243	Structure
229/233	Troy

Chapter 36

232 One night, at the . . .
Night time, and summer, in more senses than one, is nearly over. Be aware of how the description of the natural setting foreshadows the events about to erupt.

227/235	Bathsheba
229/233	Nature

233 'Will you tell him . . .'
There is a contrast here between Troy and Gabriel which the oncoming storm highlights; Gabriel, close to nature, is able to sense that danger approaches and that the exposed ricks which represent the wealth of the farm need to be secured. Troy, lacking in country sense and unconcerned about the potential dangers, ignores Gabriel's advice.

228/236	Gabriel
232/236	Nature
231/234	Troy

234 Bathsheba put her hand . . .
How does Troy show his enjoyment of the power in his new-found status as male head of the farm? Earlier in the chapter he suggested changes needed to be made at the farmhouse, here he makes a much more dangerous change – despite the pleas of Bathsheba.

219/238	Rural community
233/238	Troy

235 Bathsheba indignantly left . . .
What does it suggest about Bathsheba's changed role that she leaves the barn with the other women?

232/237	Bathsheba

236 This was enough . . .
'Every voice in nature was unanimous in bespeaking change' – the indications noted in the previous chapter of nature 'gathering her forces' for an onslaught on the farm will now find their fulfilment.

233/237	Gabriel
233/237	Nature

237 Seven hundred and fifty . . .
How accurate is the suggestion that all the wheat is in danger because of the 'instability of woman'? Is 'instability' a reasonable assessment of Bathsheba's main weakness? Note Gabriel's reaction. Well in tune with nature, balanced in his love for Bathsheba, he determines to save the ricks, and Bathsheba's fortune – despite Troy.

235/239	Bathsheba
230/238	Character
236/239	Gabriel
236/239	Nature

238 To be just . . .
The drunken state of the farm workers demonstrates Troy's headstrong irresponsibility. His insistence that drink should 'be the bond of their union' is in stark contrast to the bonds that Bathsheba forged when she first took on the responsibility of the farm.

237/240	Character
234/244	Rural community
234/247	Troy

Chapter 37

	Characters and ideas previous/next comment	

239 A light flapped . . .
This is another of the great natural scenes, and again one where Bathsheba and Gabriel are set apart from the other characters of the novel. Notice how they join together to save the farm, and the lightning throws their shadows over everything. Just as their shadows are enormous so they both seem to grow as characters, with Bathsheba coming face to face with the realities of her situation.

237/240	Bathsheba
237/240	Nature
237/244	Gabriel

240 Before Oak had laid . . .
Gabriel's description of Bathsheba as 'the only venturesome' woman in the parish indicates the deep regard he still has for her, and says something about her independent spirit. Although foolhardy decisions brought her to this distressing situation, that same independent and determined spirit will enable her to rise above the problems she has brought upon herself.

239/241	Bathsheba
238/242	Character
239/244	Nature

241 'Gabriel,' she said, in . . .
Note the quiet, determined way in which Bathsheba gains Gabriel's undivided attention. After the angry vigour of the storm, it is as if a new element has entered Bathsheba's life. What does this conversation tell us of Bathsheba's state of mind and the extent of her realization of the disastrous actions she has undertaken?

| 240/242 | Bathsheba |
| 239/242 | Gabriel |

242 'I must, I suppose . . .'
This time, her impetuosity drives her to voice the truth of the reason for her marriage to Troy—'jealousy and distraction'. Note her changing and developing character as she accepts responsibility for her actions. Her worry that Gabriel might 'be lost' and her thanks for his devotion indicate that perhaps at last she is beginning to recognize the sterling qualities of Gabriel's character.

241/247	Bathsheba
240/244	Character
241/244	Gabriel

Chapter 38

243 Oak suddenly remembered . . .
As the author points out, eight months before Gabriel had been engaged in a desperate battle to save the ricks from fire. This time the elements have threatened them with water. Note that previously Bathsheba had been very much the onlooker, this time she worked with Gabriel—perhaps a good omen for the future?

| 231/247 | Structure |

244 It was about seven . . .
Gabriel, like his name, Oak, is not destroyed by the storm, but is at one with natural forces. That Troy should walk past the ricks indifferent as to their fate is not perhaps surprising. But that the rustics should do the same is a measure of how disruptive Troy's presence has been to the usual priorities of these men's lives.

242/245	Character
242/246	Gabriel
240/252	Nature
238/263	Rural community

245 'Overlooked them,' repeated . . .
How does Boldwood 'forgetting his husbandry' serve to heighten and illustrate his mental disintegration?

| 230/246 | Boldwood |
| 244/248 | Character |

246 'But the real truth of . . .'
There is a sense of pathos about Boldwood. Contrast the strong, silent
individual that Bathsheba first saw at the Corn Exchange, with this broken
man, confiding his grief to Gabriel. Note also the contrast between Gabriel
and Boldwood in the nature of their love for Bathsheba. Gabriel's is clear-
sighted, recognizing her weaknesses and strengths, Boldwood's is warped,
concentrating on the disappointment to himself. The biblical images he uses
of a man smitten by the Lord tend to reinforce this view.

245/285	Boldwood
244/260	Gabriel
223/249	Love and marriage

Chapter 39

247 One Saturday evening . . .
Evening sees the signs of a growing rift between Bathsheba and Troy,
symbolized in their physical separation as they travel uphill, and in
Bathsheba's listlessness contrasted with this 'erect, well-made young man'.

242/248	Bathsheba
243/250	Structure
238/248	Troy

248 One Saturday evening . . .
Troy's irresponsible cruelty to the horse 'as a recreation' indicates the
unthinking and cruel streak in his personality. His casual use of Bathsheba's
money for gambling bodes ill for the future.

245/249	Character
247/249	Bathsheba
247/249	Troy

249 A flash of . . .
Despite some appearances to the contrary, this 'flash of indignation' on
Bathsheba's part and her resolution, show she is not totally bowed. You may
recall that in chapter 4, she suggested she wanted someone 'to tame' her.
Has she found the right man to do it, and is she tamed? Or does she not
require taming in the sense of breaking her spirit but rather a taming of her
impetuosity and vanity with the directing of her energies into a more
productive channel?

248/258	Bathsheba
246/295	Love and marriage
248/251	Troy
248/255	Character

250 A woman appeared . . .
Again we meet the shadowy figure of Fanny. Absent from the action for a
while, she reappears at a crucial time in Bathsheba's and Troy's relationship.
Do you recall how a little while ago Bathsheba was suggesting to Gabriel she
would end up in the workhouse? We now see in Fanny's appearance a living
testimony to the thoughtlessness and selfishness of Troy which could well
lead to Bathsheba's words being fulfilled.

223/251	Fanny
247/257	Structure

251 'Stay where you are, . . .'
Troy delays in helping Fanny by first sending away the gig in which she
could have ridden, and then by being too busy to see her until Monday.
What is Troy's first concern in each of these actions?

250/252	Fanny
249/255	Troy

Chapter 40

252 For a considerable time . . .
Note how the dark, moonless night, with cloud 'shutting out every speck of
heaven', stresses Fanny's hopeless situation.

251/253	Fanny
244/253	Nature

253 The Casterbridge lights . . .
The reader is presented with a scene which touches the very depths of human suffering. It is nature that provides as it were the 'funeral bell' – 'that acme and sublimation of all dismal sounds, the bark of a fox'. Note how a few pages on it is a dog that helps Fanny on the final steps of her last journey. At the end, Fanny listens for human sounds – only to avoid them.

254 'I stoned him away . . .'
With cruel irony, the only being to help Fanny, the dog, was stoned away from the workhouse door for its pains.

Chapter 41

255 'Bathsheba, could you . . .'
Troy will lie about money and Fanny to his wife. To what extent is he fulfilling the description of his character which was presented in chapter 25?

256 Troy for the moment . . .
Are we here seeing a new side to Troy? What is it that he does not want Bathsheba to 'inspect'. The anxiety upon Troy's face has already been noted.

257 'I must go, in . . .'
Gabriel requires no watch – nature is his timepiece. Troy has a watch in which to keep a lock of Fanny's hair; a watch which he both gave and as quickly took back from Bathsheba. You will recall how he took a lock of Bathsheba's hair, in a moment of vanity: this piece presumably means much more to him, but ironically will contribute to his undoing.

258 'This is all I get . . .'
Bathsheba's pleading indicates the depths of misery to which she has sunk. Neither she nor Troy can appreciate the prophetic nature of his words – 'women will be the death of me'. Is the irony of this exclamation also that he is directly to blame for the death of Fanny? Is there any way in which she could be said to be at least partly responsible for her own fate?

259 Directly he had gone . . .
Is there any trace left of the vanity which was so characteristic of the Bathsheba we knew at the beginning of the novel?

260 After breakfast she . . .
Gabriel, the man whose love she had at first rejected is now much more in Bathsheba's thoughts. His sterling and reliable qualities have seen him through all the trials so far, leaving him stronger and if possible even more enduring. No wonder that Bathsheba, in the midst of her turmoil should start to turn to the one stable and dependable influence she has in her life.

261 'Indeed I shall not . . .'
In a perverse sort of way is there indeed a sense in which Fanny 'belongs' to Bathsheba? Is she somehow driven to attempt to make amends to Fanny for her husband's irresponsible behaviour – however unknowingly?

Characters and ideas previous/next comment	
252/254	Fanny
252/254	Nature
253/261	Fanny
253/265	Nature
251/256	Character
249/257	Troy
255/259	Character
255/257	Troy
250/264	Structure
256/272	Troy
249/259	Bathsheba
218/268	Fate and irony
258/260	Bathsheba
256/269	Character
259/261	Bathsheba
246/267	Gabriel
260/262	Bathsheba
254/263	Fanny

262 Bathsheba, still unhappy, . . .
At last the significance of the past few day's events begins to break with
some force upon Bathsheba's perceptions. The lock of hair, a symbol of
Troy's love for Fanny, will be his undoing.

Chapter 42

263 As the clock . . .
Joseph Poorgrass is entrusted to bring back the coffin but his drinking on the
way delays the funeral. This creates time for Bathsheba to learn the truth.

264 One of the men . . .
Note how the author directs our attention to the 'few other words' and then
as quickly lessens their import by leaving the suggestion in our minds that
the words were but a single epitaph – 'we believe they do these things more
tenderly now . . .'.

265 The afternoon drew . . .
Nature reflects the sadness of the occasion. The sky was closed in by 'dark
spongy forms', and the first fog of autumn drew down upon the waggon.

266 Going down into . . .
It is a little while since there was an interlude in the narrative where the
rustics could play their part. Now they are given free rein to comment on
Fanny's death and give their views on religious practice. Their relaxed,
though perhaps irresponsible, view of their priorities lends a touch of
humour to an occasion that was fast becoming very melodramatic, though
the drama involved in Fanny's death is yet to be fully played out.

267 Suddenly, as in a . . .
It is only at the end of this chapter that the author suddenly explains the
mystery of the 'few other words' that were written on Fanny's coffin.
Gabriel's efforts to conceal the truth from Bathsheba leaves the reader
anxious to discover whether his efforts will be at all successful. Certainly,
the fact that the coffin is lodged in Bathsheba's house leaves the success of
his efforts in some doubt!

Chapter 43

268 Bathsheba was lonely and . . .
Has Bathsheba had some strange premonition about this coffin that she
should now suffer the 'gravity of a further misgiving'? Note how a few
paragraphs on we may guess at the content of the rumour which Liddy
whispers in her ear by the agitated manner of her response and the reference
to 'only one name' written on the coffin cover.

269 She suddenly felt a . . .
Note how Bathsheba is finally coming to appreciate the strength of Gabriel's
durability. Consider whether Bathsheba recognizes that the inward-looking

Characters and ideas	
previous/next comment	
261/263	Bathsheba
262/268	Bathsheba
261/267	Fanny
244/266	Rural community
257/267	Structure
254/274	Nature
263/305	Rural community
263/268	Fanny
260/269	Gabriel
264/270	Structure
263/269	Bathsheba
267/271	Fanny
258/282	Fate and irony
268/270	Bathsheba
259/281	Character

	Characters and ideas previous/next comment

natures of herself and Boldwood are their weaknesses, whilst Gabriel's strength lay in his unselfish consideration of others.

267/270   Gabriel

270 She flung a cloak . . .
Events have come full circle. There was a time when Gabriel stood outside a window looking in on Bathsheba. Now, Bathsheba is the wanderer in the night and Gabriel is inside his home. Note her envy of the 'atmosphere of content' which came from Gabriel's home – in stark contrast to her own tormented house. She will however, very shortly draw strength from the scene she has witnessed, especially her view of Gabriel praying.

269/271   Bathsheba
267/278   Structure
269/287   Gabriel

271 Bathsheba became at this . . .
In her terror of the moment Bathsheba grasps at the image of Gabriel praying to help her retain her sanity. Like him, she kneels and prays. Despite their physical separation, at this moment she and Gabriel are closer than they have ever been.

270/272   Bathsheba
268/279   Fanny

272 What Troy did was . . .
How is Troy's rare moment of tenderness in the novel so damaging to Bathsheba? The depths to which Bathsheba had sunk in her passion for Troy finds its fulfilment in this wild scene before Fanny's coffin.

271/273   Bathsheba
257/273   Troy

273 'And that this woman . . .'
How accurate is Bathsheba's accusation? Is there any difference in her and Fanny's circumstances with regard to their relationship with Troy? Consider Troy's rebuttal and the reasons he gives and whether he is at all justified in blaming Bathsheba's 'face' and 'coquetries'. Troy's brutal insensitivity to Bathsheba's suffering is measured in his words to Fanny, 'but never mind, . . . you are my very, very wife!' You might like to consider who Troy is feeling more sorry for, Fanny or himself?

272/274   Bathsheba
272/279   Troy

Chapter 44

274 Bathsheba went along . . .
In this and subsequent paragraphs note how Bathsheba's mood is reflected in the images which nature provides for the viewer.

273/275   Bathsheba
265/275   Nature

275 There was an opening . . .
Note how at the end of this paragraph Bathsheba 'arose with a tremor' at the thought of having passed the night here. Was the 'brink' not just physical but also mental?

274/277   Bathsheba
274/276   Nature

276 Bathsheba never forgot . . .
Liddy has always been at Bathsheba's side – sometimes a little ill-used, but always there. Here she seems to present a picture of innocence triumphing over the foul nature of the evil she has passed over. 'Liddy did not sink' and she seems to represent a hopeful sign to Bathsheba.

275/278   Nature

277 'Yes. Some of those we . . .'
Note the touch of humour in Bathsheba's choice of reading – hardly cheerful

275/283   Bathsheba

titles, but it does indicate her inner strength which will be needed for the trials to come. To what extent would you say that Bathsheba is a changed woman?

278 The sun went down . . .
Notice the ominous colour of the 'blood-red' sun. Nature seems to be providing a warning that the drama is not yet resolved and the noise of lads playing is suddenly silenced by the arrival of the undertakers.

| 276/287 | Nature |
| 270/284 | Structure |

Chapter 45

279 On reaching Casterbridge . . .
This flashback to the events before he discovered Fanny was dead provide us with the background to Troy's whereabouts. The irony of his being kept waiting and the anger he displays, and then much later in the day wondering if perhaps she had been ill, provide a wry comment on his actions. He knew she was ill when he and Bathsheba met her on the road, but his anger at being made to wait, his concern for his own self outweighed any possibility of him thinking about Fanny.

| 271/282 | Fanny |
| 273/280 | Troy |

280 It was all the money . . .
There is a certain grim humour in the description of Troy's use of the money he had gathered together to give Fanny while she lived.

| 279/281 | Troy |

281 Troy, in his prostration . . .
Note the commentary on Troy's actions and the motives that drive him on. Would you agree with the analysis? If you do can you refer to incidents in the novel which would support your view?

| 269/283 | Character |
| 280/282 | Troy |

Chapter 46

282 He entered the gravel . . .
If Troy had left the scene immediately after planting his flowers, he could have gone content in the knowledge that he had left a lasting and beautiful remembrance of his love for Fanny, and we would not have been able, perhaps, to judge otherwise. However, having slept the night in the church porch he is there to see the total destruction of his efforts to beautify Fanny's grave. Note how a few paragraphs on he gives up the struggle and leaves. Does this also mark the end of his remorse?

268/285	Fate and irony
281/284	Troy
279/0	Fanny

283 Oak saw her, and . . .
In this final paragraph of the chapter, how is Bathsheba's developing maturity indicated?

| 277/285 | Bathsheba |
| 281/286 | Character |

Chapter 47

284 Troy wandered along . . .
Troy's disappearance, like Fanny's, will be a temporary matter. Conveniently his removal from the Weatherbury scene and presumed death,

| 278/288 | Structure |
| 282/289 | Troy |

will allow for the movement of the story to its climax with Boldwood once more coming to the fore in Bathsheba's life.

Chapter 48

285 'I have some awkward . . .'
Fate places Boldwood on the spot to assist Bathsheba when she is informed of Troy's drowning. Boldwood is naturally not displeased at the news! However, Bathsheba, even in her upset state, has sufficient presence of mind to decline Boldwood's offer to take her home.

283/286	Bathsheba
246/287	Boldwood
282/0	Fate and irony

286 'He was hers and . . .'
The final paragraph of this chapter perhaps marks the turning point in Bathsheba's transition from girl to mature woman as she accepts that she had no part of Troy, and is still able to keep Fanny's lock in remembrance of her.

285/287	Bathsheba
283/291	Character

Chapter 49

287 The late autumn and . . .
Notice how Hardy uses the seasons as noting a passage of time during which Gabriel enjoys increased status, Bathsheba lives apathetically and Boldwood resumes his hopes of winning her hand.

286/295	Bathsheba
278/314	Nature
285/295	Boldwood
270/296	Gabriel

Chapter 50

288 Greenhill was the . . .
Hardy's description of the sheep fair is vivid and realistic. Its animation and bustle is a contrast to the lack of action in the plot.

284/292	Structure

289 At the rear of . . .
The reintroduction of Troy to the novel, and especially at a fair to which the Weatherbury folk come will set the action into motion. The presence of Bathsheba, Boldwood and Gabriel in the same place, as well as Bathsheba's old bailiff signifies that the main strands of the plot are about to meet and be resolved.

284/290	Troy

290 And now the mild autumn . . .
It is perhaps fitting that Troy should be playing the part of Turpin – a well-known and dashing villain. It is also perhaps rather prophetic that he plays a part which involves the dashing villain getting shot.

289/291	Troy

291 She looked so charming . . .
Has Troy lost any of his vanity? His sense of shame is not merely that he should be discovered, but that he should be discovered to have fallen so low.

286/306	Character
290/293	Troy

292 Troy stood at the . . .
Can you recall another character and another occasion when Bathsheba was

288/294	Structure

spied upon through a hole? How do the motives and actions of the two 'spies' differ?

293 Bathsheba held the note . . .
Troy's audacious attempt to steal the note would suggest that his absence has not led to any change in his character.

291/301   Troy

294 Troy reached the tent . . .
The chapter ends with Troy and Pennyways disappearing into the night together. What is the only conclusion that the reader is left with?

292/298   Structure

Chapter 51

295 The keen instincts of . . .
Bathsheba's remorse at the anguish she has caused Boldwood causes her to allow too free an expression of the pity she feels for him. Certainly Boldwood interprets her attitude in such a way as to lead him to suddenly ask '. . . you will marry again some day?' Given her past experiences what should her answer have been – at least so far as Boldwood was concerned? She still seems not to have discovered the difference between pity, infatuation, and love. In this long discussion of their relationship there are repetitions of previous conversations with Boldwood.

287/296   Bathsheba
287/300   Boldwood
249/297   Love and marriage

296 One day she was led . . .
How does Bathsheba's conversation with Gabriel indicate the honesty of their relationship and her total lack of perception with regard to Gabriel's feelings and position?

295/297   Bathsheba
287/316   Gabriel

297 'Yes, you may suppose . . .'
How do Bathsheba's views on love differ from when she spoke to Gabriel in chapter 4? There is something mildly insulting to Gabriel in her concern for Boldwood and the way she feels she has damaged him as much of what she says could equally be applied to the way she has treated Gabriel.

296/299   Bathsheba
295/310   Love and marriage

Chapter 52

298 Christmas-eve came, . . .
Note how Hardy has structured this chapter. For the first time in the book we have a chapter divided in a number of short sections, each dealing with the interrelated affairs of the main characters. The first section sets the scene for the coming action, and in spite of the revelry 'a shadow seemed to move about the rooms' – suggesting that all will not go smoothly with the party.

294/304   Structure

299 Bathsheba was at . . .
Despite sitting at her mirror, Bathsheba is not at all prey to the vanity which would previously have coloured her thoughts. What is it that makes her uneasy about attending the party? Does her black dress symbolize her view of a joyless future?

297/302   Bathsheba

Characters and ideas previous/next comment

300 Boldwood was dressing . . .
Note the heightened sense of detail which affects Boldwood's judgment of his dress. His hands shake and he cannot tie his neckerchief. What other signs are there that he is in a very agitated mood?

295/303　Boldwood

301 Troy was sitting . . .
Note the judgments that Troy makes in this section of the chapter. He previously dismissed both Gabriel and Boldwood with contemptuous gifts of money. His opinion of them would appear not to have changed at all.

293/304　Troy

302 'How do I look . . .'
Is this question asked in any sense of vanity? Note how Liddy brings up the subject of marriage, in an oblique way. Do we see something prophetic in her comment 'knowing what rum things we women be' – especially with Bathsheba's reply in mind?

299/306　Bathsheba

303 'Oak,' said Boldwood . . .
Note the way that Boldwood almost seems to be putting his affairs in order. A few paragraphs on we read that Gabriel was uneasy about him, and shortly after as Boldwood looks out of the window the 'twilight was deepening to darkness' – not a very encouraging sign.

300/306　Boldwood

304 'How does this cover . . .'
As we left Boldwood in the deepening darkness of the last section, so now we meet Troy cloaking his form and features from view, neither of them very encouraging images. Note the calculating way in which Troy discusses his return and the reasons behind it. During this chapter we have seen an uneasy Bathsheba, Boldwood in a highly excited state of mind, and Troy at his most cruel and calculating – all bound for Boldwood's 'party'. The reader is left in little doubt that the various strands of the plot will find their outcome in the following chapter.

298/305　Structure
301/307　Troy

Chapter 53

305 Outside the front . . .
Note how before the tragic events of the party are allowed to commence, the rustics are brought on to voice their opinions of the possible outcome of Troy's return and the affect he had in the past on the folk of Weatherbury.

266/318　Rural community
304/308　Structure

306 'Now that's an evasion . . .'
Have you noted how much reliance Boldwood always places on the 'promises' Bathsheba made to him, or perhaps more accurately his interpretation of what he thinks are promises. Is he at all justified in thinking that he has any sort of promise from Bathsheba with regard to marriage? Much earlier in the story reference was made to Boldwood failing to flatter Bathsheba. Unfortunately, he seems to have learned his lesson too late!

302/310　Bathsheba
303/307　Boldwood
291/311　Character

307 Troy next advanced . . .
Note the emotive language in the description of Boldwood's view of Troy, 'impersonator', 'heaven's persistent irony', 'scourged', and 'snatched'. It is Troy's 'mechanical' laugh which causes Boldwood to recognize him, and it

306/309　Boldwood
304/308　Troy

seems to paralyse the whole party. Bathsheba is transfixed. Only the voice of Boldwood responds to Troy's command, and in a totally unexpected manner. What breaks the party's paralysis is Bathsheba's scream, a scream that turns Boldwood's mind and leads to the death of Troy.

306/309 Boldwood
304/308 Troy

308 Troy fell. The . . .
The shooting of Troy can be considered as the novel's climax. From now on the action falls away, with only some 'tidying up' necessary to satisfy the reader's desire to actually be told of the conclusion.

305/0 Structure
307/310 Troy

Chapter 54

309 Boldwood passed into . . .
Boldwood gives himself up. Is this an act of honour, despair, or both?

307/313 Boldwood

310 Long before this time . . .
Bathsheba moves instinctively to take Troy in her arms. Does the reader understand here that she still loves Troy? Do you sympathize with her?

306/311 Bathsheba
308/311 Troy
297/316 Love and marriage

311 'Gabriel,' she said, . . .
Bathsheba's response to the murder is one of dignity, stability, bravery, and tenderness. She has developed considerably since the novel began.

310/312 Bathsheba
306/315 Character
310/0 Troy

312 'It is all done, . . .'
Bathsheba demonstrates 'the heart of a wife'–perhaps the ultimate praise for her–in laying out her dead husband. Notice how the pace has slowed as the characters act with restraint and speak in subdued voices.

311/314 Bathsheba

Chapter 55

313 That he had been . . .
Note the pathetic evidence in Boldwood's house of 'a mind crazed with care and love'. We only now begin to appreciate the depth of Boldwood's fixation on Bathsheba and the enormous toll that her thoughtless valentine exacted.

309/0 Boldwood

Chapter 56

314 Bathsheba revived with . . .
With the emergence of spring comes new hope, and gradually we see Bathsheba turning a little to her farming concerns. Note how a few paragraphs on Bathsheba demonstrates her maturity in the choice of a resting place for Troy.

312/315 Bathsheba
287/317 Nature

| | *Characters and ideas previous/next comment* | |

315 Then they stood in . . .
Consider the change in Bathsheba in this chapter. How does she feel about running the farm, what people think of her, and Gabriel's wish to emigrate?

| 314/316 | Bathsheba |
| 311/0 | Character |

316 He accompanied her up . . .
The strength and enduring qualities of their love is stressed in the lack of 'pretty phrases'.

315/317	Bathsheba
296/317	Gabriel
310/0	Love and marriage

Chapter 57

317 It was a damp and . . .
The dreary weather makes no comment here on Gabriel and Bathsheba's happiness. As countryfolk, they have dressed to suit both the occasion and the weather.

316/0	Bathsheba
316/0	Gabriel
314/0	Nature

318 'Yes, I suppose that's . . .'
Fittingly, the novel ends with words from one of the rustics who represents the community within which all the events have taken place and where the newly married couple most surely belong.

| 305/0 | Rural community |

Characters in the novel

This is a very brief overview of each of the major characters. You should use it as a starting point for your own studies of characterization. For each of the aspects of character mentioned you should look in your text for evidence to support or contradict the views expressed here, and indeed, your own views as well.

Know the incidents and conversations which will support and enlarge upon your knowledge of each character. You will find it helpful to select a character and follow the commentary, referring always to the text to read and digest the context of the comment.

Mr Boldwood

Boldwood is a local, respected gentleman-farmer. He has dignity, and is depicted as a good neighbour: he was kind to Fanny and also to Gabriel. He is noticeably chivalrous in his attempt to save Bathsheba from finding out the truth about her husband's past. His unstable emotions surprise the reader; he is absorbed by Bathsheba's light-hearted valentine, loses his self-control and pursues her with an obsessive passion and desire to make her his wife. You should consider the reasons for this passion. Is he so besotted by his love for Bathsheba that he will do anything for her, or is his passion the result of a self-centred wish to fulfil his own desires, though not in any sexual sense? His passion, whatever its cause, leads to tragedy, and after Troy's murder he gives himself up. Is that the act of a man suffering remorse or despair? There is a difference.

Bathsheba Everdene

Bathsheba is a complex character. Her marked development is central to the progress of the novel. The early chapters stress her high-spirited independent nature, her vanity and capricious spirit. The responses she makes to Gabriel and her attitude towards him are sometimes quite irresponsible as indeed is the irresponsible way she initially deals with Boldwood. In the middle chapters she is capable, brave and self-reliant, struggling against multiplying disasters which have their origins in her earlier immaturity. Emotional immaturity leads her towards two disasters, her involvement with Boldwood and her love for Troy. As the marriage turns bitter she holds the reader's sympathy through her resourceful nature. Hardy makes it clear that Bathsheba's character suggests a woman of fine feelings and flaws. By the end of the novel she reveals an inner strength which is demonstrated by her being able to endure Troy and Fanny being buried together and by her keeping Fanny's lock of hair as a memento of the poor girl. It is this inner strength which illuminates her need and love for Gabriel who has remained true throughout her progress.

Gabriel Oak

Gabriel is the central figure in the backdrop of country life in which the novel is placed. He is skilled as shepherd and farmer; his name symbolizes strength and endurance. His love for Bathsheba is frank, realistic, and above all reliable and stable. He is unselfish, and resourceful, able to withstand misfortune in all areas of his life, love and work. Gabriel is the counterbalance of all the other major characters. Hardy has idealized this character who represents a man in harmony with the earth, and who is part of the country's legacy of agricultural traditions, values and quality of life.

You ought to consider if there is any change in his character, or whether, like an oak tree, he merely continues to grow in stature as the novel progresses. Particularly bear in mind the conversations he has with Bathsheba. What, for example, are the reasons that make him accept dismissal on one occasion, yet on another reject it outright?

Fanny Robin

Fanny, a young local country girl, waits for Troy to arrange their wedding. He seems to be willing but vague. When the appointed time arrives Fanny's naïvety is displayed by her going to the wrong church. After this Troy is angry and Fanny is doomed. She is pregnant and alone. Her exhausted trudge to the workhouse is unforgettably poignant. Her story affects all the major characters through her link with Troy to Bathsheba. Fanny's death is the climax of the story; the coffin scene is horrifying, touching and dismaying. Her character is simply drawn from her naïve honesty, and her forlorn faith in her lover. In many ways, Fanny represents the plight of the Victorian working-class female who strays outside the narrow confines of society's rules.

Troy

Troy is a fascinating blend of attractiveness and repulsiveness. Chapter 25 is devoted to a detailed description of him. His appearance is blindingly attractive to women and his dashing manner, fluent flattery and skill with a sword enable him to 'assault' his chosen female and dominate her. He seems to have strength of character but this is quickly negated, for example his frankness is soon balanced by lies, his love for Fanny is balanced by his final neglect of her and his cruel abuse of Bathsheba. He enjoys role-playing, but as master of the farm he is irresponsible and uncommitted to its well-being. In the end, any close analysis of his character and actions reveals him as an unprincipled cheat and liar. By the end of the novel he has neither changed nor developed. Are you in agreement with the last two sentences, and could you justify your opinion?

What happens in each chapter

Chapter 1   Gabriel Oak is a young bachelor farmer, a sensible, strong, hard-working man who is at one with his environment. On a December morning he sees a lovely young woman seated on a wagon amongst her belongings. He notes certain aspects of her character as she argues over a twopenny toll and later views herself with satisfaction in her mirror.

Chapter 2   Gabriel Oak has his own small sheep farm on Norcombe Hill. The landscape, sounds and sensations are strikingly described. Gabriel has a small hut from which he works, tending his flock with skill and care. During the night Gabriel notices a light coming from a small shed on a hillside. Inside are two women nursing a cow with a newly born calf. He recognizes the girl he saw in the wagon. This is the second time he has observed her without her knowing.

Chapter 3   Oak sees the girl the next morning; he observes her skill and obvious enjoyment of freedom from social restraints as she rides her horse. He returns a hat she had lost but on the days that follow she does not speak to him.

One night Gabriel falls asleep in his hut forgetting to leave a ventilator open. It is only the girl's chance and timely intervention which saves him from suffocation. In the conversation she teases him and refuses to tell him her name.

Chapter 4   Gabriel's interest in the girl develops. He decides he will ask her to be his wife. An orphaned lamb gives him the opportunity to visit her with the lamb as a gift; he intends to propose. The girl's aunt tells him she is out and that she has many suitors. Gabriel starts off for his home but Bathsheba races after him. Her intention is to explain that she is not surrounded by suitors. Gabriel misinterprets this and is encouraged to propose and outline his intentions for their life-style. Bathsheba does not relish the prospect of marriage, especially as she does not love Gabriel. She tells him he should find a rich wife who would help him. Gabriel declares he will love her till he dies though she has refused him.

Chapter 5   Time passes and Bathsheba has moved to Weatherbury, twenty miles away. Gabriel's love for her is constant but he is thankful that he is unmarried when disaster strikes and he loses his entire flock and his livelihood. There is a powerful description of the crazy dog driving the sheep over the cliff. Gabriel shoots the dog, sells his land to pay his debts and is left with what he carries.

Chapter 6   Gabriel looks for employment at Casterbridge hiring fair. He earns a little money playing his flute but still without work he sets out at night to walk to the next fair near Weatherbury. He listens to two carters talking of the vanity of a local lady who owns a farm. Gabriel sees a fire burning in the distance and goes to help. He organizes a systematic quenching of the fire. The young woman farm owner has watched him from a distance and sends words of thanks. Gabriel hopes she will offer him work. He goes to her and as she lifts her veil he recognizes her – it is Bathsheba.

Chapter 7   Bathsheba agrees to employ Gabriel as shepherd but delegates the details of hiring to her bailiff Pennyways. Gabriel is on his way to Warren's Malthouse where he plans to lodge temporarily when he meets a frail young woman on the road. She asks him not tell anyone he has seen her. Gabriel is moved by her agitation; he gives her a shilling. As he does so he notices her racing pulse.

Chapter 8   Gabriel is made welcome at the Malthouse. He learns that Bathsheba's parents are dead and that she inherited the farm from an uncle. There is lively and realistic dialogue between the local characters. They talk of Bathsheba's dismissal of her bailiff, and the disappearance of Fanny Robin, one of Bathsheba's servants. The locals speak of a soldier who was Fanny's young man. Bathsheba sends someone to Casterbridge to find out about Fanny. Gabriel goes to lodge at one of the farmworker's homes.

Chapter 9 Bathsheba is sorting out her late uncle's papers and belongings with the help of her personal maid, Liddy. A man on horseback calls; he is a neighbour, a rich farmer in his middle years, Mr Boldwood. He has come to pay his respects and to inquire after Fanny. Bathsheba does not see him as she feels she is not dressed to receive callers. The women talk of love, admirers and marriage. Liddy asks Bathsheba if she has ever had a proposal. Bathsheba admits that she has but does not name her admirer. The farm-hands arrive to collect their wages.

Chapter 10 Bathsheba informs her workers of Bailiff Pennyway's dismissal, and her intention to run the farm herself. She talks to each worker and pays the wages they are due, plus some bonuses. Gabriel is treated formally and given Cainy Ball as his under-shepherd. News is brought that Fanny Robin has left Casterbridge with a sergeant in the dragoons. Bathsheba sends this information on to Boldwood. She informs the group of workers of her intention to work hard and make her farm a success. She leaves the room with royal grace – Liddy imitates this.

Chapter 11 Fanny approaches the Melchester Barracks on a snowy night. There she communicates with Troy through a window. He is unenthusiastic about arranging their wedding and presents several delaying tactics. He agrees to call on her the next day at her lodgings.

Chapter 12 Bathsheba demonstrates her ability to carry out her farm's business as she negotiates prices at the Casterbridge Corn Exchange. All admire her with one notable exception. This is Boldwood, an unmarried, successful farmer, he seems indifferent to women.

Chapter 13 Bathsheba and Liddy decide to play the old superstitious game which uses a Bible and key as means of telling the future. Marks on the pages suggest it has been used for this purpose many times. Liddy, being aware that Boldwood is on Bathsheba's mind, suggests that instead of directing the valentine she is writing to a small child, she sends it to Boldwood. This is undertaken in a spirit of jest.

Chapter 14 Boldwood is deeply affected by the valentine and ponders about the mystery woman who sent it. He is unable to sleep and takes a walk at dawn. He meets a postman who gives him, by mistake, a letter for Gabriel. After opening it Boldwood sets off to make an apology to its rightful owner.

Chapter 15 Some farm workers are in the local tavern talking about Bathsheba's supposed inability to run the estate as she is a woman. They grant that she is educated and clever, but criticize her vanity and extravagance. Gabriel warns them all that they will have to reckon with him if they speak badly of her again. Boldwood arrives and gives Gabriel his letter. This is from Fanny Robin. She returns his money and tells him she will soon be married to Sergeant Troy. She believes him to be a man of honour. When Gabriel shows Boldwood the letter Boldwood doubts Troy's integrity. Boldwood shows Gabriel the valentine. Gabriel is able to identify the handwriting as Bathsheba's.

Chapter 16 Troy waits in All Saints' Church for Fanny to arrive for their wedding ceremony. Over half an hour passes as Troy grows more embarrassed and humiliated. As he leaves Fanny arrives having waited at the wrong church. Troy in anger refuses to arrange a definite place or time for another ceremony.

Chapter 17 Boldwood is obsessed now by thoughts of Bathsheba. At the cornmarket on Saturday morning he gazes rapturously at her and enquires of others as to whether she is considered to be a great beauty. Bathsheba feels pleased to have attracted him but regrets that it was the foolish valentine which brought this about. They do not speak.

Chapter 18 Boldwood is a man of some importance in the parish. His land adjoins Bathsheba's. He sees her working in a field and feels compelled to approach her and speak. Shyness prevents him but his presence has been noted by Bathsheba; it causes her embarrassment. Gabriel senses her change of mood. Bathsheba determines to give Boldwood no further reason to think she is interested in him.

Chapter 19   Boldwood decides he must speak to Bathsheba so seeks her out when she is watching the sheep-washing. He passionately declares his love and proposes. Bathsheba tries to refuse him but feels sorry for him and so tells him she will think about it – this leaves hope in Boldwood's heart.

Chapter 20   Bathsheba, though not in love with Boldwood, knows that a marriage to him would be financially and socially advantageous. Even so she is doubtful whether it would be a wise move. She enjoys her independent control of the farm and does not feel the need for marriage. She asks Gabriel for his opinion while they are grinding shears together. Gabriel's candid reply makes Bathsheba angry and she dismisses him.

Chapter 21   The next day Bathsheba's sheep fall ill; they have wandered into a field of clover which when eaten by sheep distends their stomachs, ultimately causing death. This needs very skilled and speedy treatment. Gabriel is the only man in the locality able to cure them. Gabriel refuses to help unless he is asked politely. Bathsheba has to plead with him. He cures most of the flock. Bathsheba asks him to stay on as shepherd and he agrees.

Chapter 22   Early June is sheep-shearing time. Bathsheba watches; Oak's speed and skill impress her but the atmosphere changes with the arrival of Boldwood. Bathsheba goes out with Boldwood to view his flock. The farm workers conclude that there will be a marriage soon. Gabriel disputes this.

Chapter 23   The sheep-shearing supper is ready. Bathsheba invites Gabriel to sit at the head of the table. He has to give up this place on Boldwood's arrival. There is traditional music and singing; all make a contribution to this. Later, in the farmhouse, Boldwood again declares his love. Bathsheba promises to consider marrying him and will give her answer by harvest time. Boldwood is made happy by this.

Chapter 24   After the shearing supper Bathsheba makes her nightly round of the estate. Passing through the fir plantation she meets a man and the hem of her dress is caught in his spur. The man is a soldier – Sergeant Troy. His dashing, teasing manner both distresses and enchants Bathsheba. She runs home where Liddy tells her his history and Bathsheba feels she might have been too harsh with him.

Chapter 25   This chapter centres upon a detailed description of Troy. He emerges as a man who looks neither forward nor back but pursues gratification in the present. He lacks finer feelings, lies to women, and relies on flattery and his dashing air of reckless charm. He is not really evil, but his wrong-doing results from his impulsive actions and lack of moral discrimination. The description places Troy in direct contrast with Gabriel. At the end of the chapter Troy offers his services to Bathsheba, helping with the haymaking.

Chapter 26   Troy flatters and teases Bathsheba. She in turn teases and accuses him of pretending. Suddenly he produces a gold watch and gives it to her, declaring that he loves her. At this moment it seems he is truly attracted to her. Bathsheba is confused by his advances, refuses the gift but does accept his offer of help in her fields.

Chapter 27   Chance takes a hand when Bathsheba is having difficulty with a hive of bees. Troy arrives on the scene and is able to do the job for her after she has dressed him in her protective clothing. Troy offers to demonstrate his sword drill to her. After refusing she is persuaded to meet him in secret.

Chapter 28   Troy astonishes and dazzles Bathsheba with his dexterity and magnetism. In a ferny hollow the sword drill becomes a direct confrontation between Troy the man and Bathsheba the woman. Bathsheba is totally dominated by Troy's performance. His kiss leaves her stirred. From this scene onward Bathsheba no longer dictates the action in their relationship.

Chapter 29   Gabriel wants to speak to Bathsheba about her involvement with Troy. They meet one evening and he speaks about marriage to Boldwood. Bathsheba informs him there will be no marriage and she is angered by Gabriel's view that Troy is unworthy of her. In defence of Troy Bathsheba says he goes to church regularly but enters unobserved by a side door. Bathsheba would like to dismiss Gabriel but is reminded by him how much she needs his skilled labour. They part, she to meet Troy, he to the church where he examines the side door. It has not been opened for years. Troy has been lying.

Chapter 30   Troy is leaving for Bath. Bathsheba goes home and writes to Boldwood saying she will not marry him. On overhearing her servants discussing the probability of her marrying Troy, she tells them she hates him, but then defends him. She confesses to Liddy privately that she is in love with Troy and asks for reassurance that he is good. Liddy promises not to tell anyone of Bathsheba's feelings.

Chapter 31   Next morning while out walking Bathsheba meets Boldwood. He repeats his declaration of love but, though Bathsheba feels regret for her silly action and pities him, she will not change her mind. When she admits that Troy is the man who has her affection, Boldwood is enraged; he threatens Troy. All Bathsheba's thoughts are for Troy's safety.

Chapter 32   Noises in the night suggest someone is stealing a horse. Gabriel and a fellow worker pursue the thief on horses borrowed from Boldwood. The 'thief' is revealed as Bathsheba herself who has on impulse decided to go to Troy in Bath. She sends her workers home. It is Bathsheba's intention to warn Troy of Boldwood's desire for revenge and then not to see him again.

Chapter 33   Bathsheba is away from the farm a week and then sends a note to say she will return after a few more days. Another week passes. News is brought by Cain, Gabriel's assistant who has been in Bath. Bathsheba and Troy have been seen walking arm-in-arm. Oak says nothing but is upset by this news.

Chapter 34   That evening Bathsheba returns. Boldwood calls wishing to apologize for his behaviour; he knows nothing of Bathsheba's visit to Bath. Boldwood meets Troy and tries to bribe him to leave Bathsheba alone and to marry Fanny. When Bathsheba is seen looking for Troy, Boldwood is possessed by grief and anger at their intimacy. He then offers Troy money to marry Bathsheba in order to keep her good name. Troy discloses that he and Bathsheba were married in Bath and throws the money at Boldwood. Boldwood resorts to threats once more and spends the night tramping the hills all alone.

Chapter 35   The next morning Troy appears at an upper window of Bathsheba's house and speaks to Gabriel and another farm worker. They realize that he must have married their mistress, Bathsheba. Gabriel is very upset and knows this hasty marriage will ultimately cause Bathsheba heartache. He resolves to cover up his feelings for her sake. When they see Boldwood he, in contrast, is openly expressing his anguish and his face clearly shows the appalling sorrow which he feels.

Chapter 36   At the end of August there is a harvest celebration at the farm. Troy is now the master but he is irresponsible. Gabriel knows a storm is on the way and warns Troy that the ricks should be covered. Troy takes no notice and orders brandy to be given to the farm workers and sends their women to bed. On his way home Gabriel sees that he must cover the ricks himself if they are not be to ruined. There is no one sober enough to help so he works, with difficulty, alone.

Chapter 37   The storm breaks. Gabriel alone is trying to cover the ricks. Bathsheba arrives on the scene. She is grateful to Gabriel and bitterly disappointed that Troy has let her and the farm down. Bathsheba clearly realizes her husband is not the man she thought him to be. She confides in Gabriel that she married Troy when he made her jealous in Bath. Bathsheba goes back to the house deeply grateful to Gabriel for his loyalty and dependability.

Chapter 38   As the rain pours down the drunken men wake and go to their homes. Gabriel finishes his job and as he walks home he meets Boldwood. Boldwood, too, has failed to cover his ricks and they have been ruined in the storm. He confides in Gabriel the extent of his misery over Bathsheba but he wishes the locals to know there was never an engagement as he fears their mockery.

Chapter 39   It is October and Bathsheba and Troy are coming home from the market at Casterbridge. Troy has been losing money at the races but when Bathsheba confronts him with this he tells her she has lost all her spirit. They pass a young woman on the road – it is Fanny but Bathsheba is ignorant of her identity. Fanny faints on hearing Troy's voice. He sends Bathsheba ahead and says he will assist the woman. Troy then does what he can for Fanny; he gives her the little money he has left and arranges to meet her on Monday morning. When he returns to Bathsheba he admits to knowing the young woman but not by name.

Chapter 40   This chapter describes Fanny's struggle to walk the last miles into Casterbridge to the workhouse. Her only helper is a large dog who supports her agonized steps. At the workhouse door the dog is stoned away.

Chapter 41   Bathsheba and Troy quarrel openly and both regret their marriage. Troy argues over money; Bathsheba is jealous of his feelings for the strange woman who was very beautiful. A lock of hair – not Bathsheba's – is in Troy's watch case. Bathsheba regrets giving up her freedom so hastily. On Monday news is brought that Fanny Robin is dead. Bathsheba sends Poorgrass, a farm worker, to collect her body. Bathsheba makes enquiries and learns that Fanny had been following her lover – a soldier in Troy's regiment – and that her hair was golden, the colour of the lock in Troy's watch.

Chapter 42   Fanny's coffin is collected from the workhouse by the rustic Poorgrass. On the way home to the farm he stops at the Buck's Head Inn, where he has far too much to drink. Gabriel finds him and drives the wagon and its sad load home. The delay results in it being too late for the funeral to be held that day so Bathsheba says the coffin must be brought into the house for the night. Gabriel, in order to spare Bathsheba's feelings, rubs out the words 'and child' from the names marked on the coffin.

Chapter 43   As Bathsheba sits up waiting for Troy to come home Liddy tells her of the rumour in the village, that Fanny died having a child. Bathsheba goes to visit Gabriel hoping for advice but she changes her mind and returns home. She unscrews the coffin and sees the truth: there lie Fanny and her baby. Bathsheba prays. Filled with grief and jealousy, she arranges flowers inside the coffin. Troy arrives on the scene and torn by remorse, sadness and guilt he kisses Fanny and brutally rejects Bathsheba. In despair, Bathsheba runs from the house.

Chapter 44   Bathsheba spends the night in a wood. In the early morning Liddy finds her and persuades her to return to the house now that Troy has gone out and the coffin is about to be moved to the churchyard. Bathsheba goes into the house once the coffin has gone. She stays in the attic. Liddy informs her that a splendid tombstone has been put in the churchyard, but the donor is unknown.

Chapter 45   Hardy describes Troy's actions and thoughts after Bathsheba ran away. He had put the lid on the coffin, anguished all night and then collected all the money he could and departed for Casterbridge. There he ordered a magnificent tombstone for Fanny. Later, in the evening, he planted flowers on Fanny's grave by the light of a lantern. It began to rain and Troy sheltered in the church porch. He fell asleep there.

Chapter 46   During the heavy rain that night the rain water washes from the church roof through the guttering with its ornate, ugly gargoyle, down onto Fanny's grave. It is ruined. Troy looks upon the works of fate, turns his back on the grave and leaves. Bathsheba and Gabriel, who have gone to see Fanny's grave separately, meet there and together attempt to replant the flowers and put to rights the damage done by the water spout.

Chapter 47   Troy arrives at Budmouth on the coast. He intends to take a swim but is carried out to sea by the tide. Good luck saves him, in the form of the crew of a passing ship.

Chapter 48   As the days pass Bathsheba feels she will lose her farm as Troy will be unable to pay the rent. Troy has not returned. At the market she is informed that Troy has drowned. Bathsheba does not really believe this but at the shock of the news she faints. Boldwood is there and he supports her in his arms. Bathsheba returns home. She still doubts the validity of the reports of Troy's drowning but later thinks it might be t rue.

Chapter 49   Almost a year passes. Gabriel is made bailiff. He also looks after Boldwood's lower farm. Thus Gabriel's fortunes rise but he still lives a simple life. Boldwood again hopes to persuade Bathsheba to marry him. He is prepared to wait for her – she would be free to remarry seven years after her husband's disappearance.

Chapter 50   Bathsheba and Boldwood take flocks to Greenhill Sheep Fair. Gabriel and Cain Ball attend. There are entertainments at the fair. Troy is a performer in the circus. The narrative tells of Troy's wandering. He is now playing the role of Dick Turpin. Bathsheba watches his performance without recognizing him. Pennyways, her former bailiff, does and gives her a note to inform her. While she is talking to Boldwood Troy manages to snatch the note before she has read it.

Chapter 51   On the journey home from the fair Boldwood rides his horse beside Bathsheba's gig. He asks her again about marriage. She promises to give him a decision by Christmas. Some weeks pass. Bathsheba talks to Gabriel who is sensible in his advice. He says nothing of his love for her.

Chapter 52   Boldwood is to give a Christmas party. Bathsheba feels that he is playing host with her in mind and she feels uncomfortable. Boldwood is cheerfully anticipating the event. In Casterbridge Troy and Pennyways make plans. Troy will confront Bathsheba. He is more concerned with sharing her money and property, than in returning to his wife.

Chapter 53   The rustics have heard rumours that Troy is in Casterbridge but they are undecided about going to the party to tell Bathsheba. Troy eavesdrops on Oak who is discussing Boldwood's obsession. At the party Bathsheba is preparing to leave. Boldwood seeks her out and persuades her to agree to marry him at the end of the six-year period. He gives her a ring. Just as Bathsheba is leaving Troy appears to claim her. Boldwood takes a gun and shoots Troy. He is stopped from killing himself so leaves the house and walks into the night.

Chapter 54   Boldwood walks into Casterbridge and gives himself up at the gaol. In Boldwood's hall Bathsheba holds Troy's body and sends Gabriel to find a doctor. When the surgeon arrives he finds that Bathsheba has left. She has had Troy's body taken home where she alone has laid out Troy in preparation for his burial. Bathsheba collapses and Liddy hears her mistress pass the night in self-recrimination and misery.

Chapter 55   Boldwood is sent for trial the next March. There is evidence of his mental instability. His obsessive desire to have Bathsheba as his wife is highlighted when a hoard of jewels and expensive clothes are found in a locked room in his house. These are all labelled with the name Bathsheba Boldwood. Though Boldwood pleads guilty and the death sentence is passed, the local people petition the Home Secretary. This is successful and Boldwood is imprisoned for life.

Chapter 56   It is August. Bathsheba has kept alone for months. One day she visits the churchyard where Troy and Fanny are buried in the same grave. Oak meets her there and informs her that he is planning to go away to California next spring. Throughout autumn Gabriel avoids seeing Bathsheba, something which she finds disturbing. After Christmas Gabriel's letter of resignation arrives. Bathsheba realizes she cannot manage without him and so goes to see him. Gabriel states frankly that he is leaving because local gossips say he is only staying in hopes of her marrying him. Eventually she intimates that marriage might be possible. Oak has never asked her since he was refused at the start of the novel.

Chapter 57   On a misty morning Bathsheba and Gabriel marry very quietly with only two witnesses present. That evening the couple are sitting quietly when the villages gather outside to express their goodwill. They good-naturedly refuse refreshment so Gabriel sends food and drink for them to the Malthouse so they can drink a toast. The novel ends on a note of peaceful harmony.

Coursework and preparing for the examination

If you wish to gain a certificate in English literature then there is no substitute for studying the text/s on which you are to be examined. If you cannot be bothered to do that, then neither this guide nor any other will be of use to you.

Here we give advice on studying the text, writing a good essay, producing coursework, and sitting the examination. However, if you meet problems you should ask your teacher for help.

Studying the text

No, not just read – study. You must read your text at least twice. Do not dismiss it if you find a first reading difficult or uninteresting. Approach the text with an open mind and you will often find a second reading more enjoyable. When you become a more experienced reader enjoyment usually follows from a close study of the text, when you begin to appreciate both what the author is saying and the skill with which it is said.

Having read the text, you must now study it. We restrict our remarks here to novels and plays, though much of what is said can also be applied to poetry.

1 You will know in full detail all the major incidents in your text, **why**, **where** and **when** they happen, **who** is involved, **what** leads up to them and what follows.

2 You must show that you have an **understanding of the story**, the **characters**, and the **main ideas** which the author is exploring.

3 In a play you must know what happens in each act, and more specifically the organization of the scene structure – how one follows from and builds upon another. Dialogue in both plays and novels is crucial. You must have a detailed knowledge of the major dialogues and soliloquies and the part they play in the development of plot, and the development and drawing of character.

4 When you write about a novel you will not normally be expected to quote or to refer to specific lines but references to incidents and characters must be given, and they must be accurate and specific.

5 In writing about a play you will be expected both to paraphrase dialogue and quote specific lines, always provided, of course, that they are actually contributing something to your essay!

To gain full marks in coursework and/or in an examination you will also be expected to show your own reaction to, and appreciation of, the text studied. The teacher or examiner always welcomes those essays which demonstrate the student's own thoughtful response to the text. Indeed, questions often specify such a requirement, so do participate in those classroom discussions, the debates, class dramatizations of all or selected parts of your text, and the many other activities which enable a class to share and grow in their understanding and feeling for literature.

Making notes
A half-hearted reading of your text, or watching the 'film of the book' will not give you the necessary knowledge to meet the above demands.

As you study the text jot down sequences of events; quotations of note; which events precede and follow the part you are studying; the characters involved; what the part being studied contributes to the plot and your understanding of character and ideas.

Write single words, phrases and short sentences which can be quickly reviewed and which will help you to gain a clear picture of the incident being studied. Make your notes neat and orderly, with headings to indicate chapter, scene, page, incident, character, etc, so that you can quickly find the relevant notes or part of the text when revising.

Writing the essay

Good essays are like good books, in miniature; they are thought about, planned, logically structured, paragraphed, have a clearly defined pattern and development of thought, and are presented clearly – and with neat writing! All of this will be to no avail if the tools you use, i.e. words, and the skill with which you put them together to form your sentences and paragraphs are severely limited.

How good is your general and literary vocabulary? Do you understand and can you make appropriate use of such terms as 'soliloquy', 'character', 'plot', 'mood', 'dramatically effective', 'comedy', 'allusion', 'humour', 'imagery', 'irony', 'paradox', 'anti-climax', 'tragedy'? These are all words which examiners have commented on as being misunderstood by students.

Do you understand 'metaphor', 'simile', 'alliteration'? Can you say what their effect is on you, the reader, and how they enable the author to express himself more effectively than by the use of a different literary device? If you cannot, you are employing your time ineffectively by using them.

You are writing an English literature essay and your writing should be literate and appropriate. Slang, colloquialisms and careless use of words are not tolerated in such essays.

Essays for coursework

The exact number of essays you will have to produce and their length will vary; it depends upon the requirements of the examination board whose course you are following, and whether you will be judged solely on coursework or on a mixture of coursework and examination.

As a guide, however your course is structured, you will be required to provide a folder containing at least ten essays, and from that folder approximately five will be selected for moderation purposes. Of those essays, one will normally have been done in class-time under conditions similar to those of an examination. The essays must cover the complete range of course requirements and be the unaided work of the student. One board specifies that these pieces of continuous writing should be a minimum of 400 words long, and another, a minimum of 500 words long. Ensure that you know what is required for your course, and do not aim for the minimum amount – write a full essay then prune it down if necessary.

Do take care over the presentation of your final folder of coursework. There are many devices on the market which will enable you to bind your work neatly, and in such a way that you can easily insert new pieces. Include a 'Contents' page and a front and back cover to keep your work clean. Ring binders are unsuitable items to hand in for **final** assessment purposes as they are much too bulky.

What sort of coursework essays will you be set? All boards lay down criteria similar to the following for the range of student response to literature that the coursework must cover.

Work must demonstrate that the student:

1 shows an understanding not only of surface meaning but also of a deeper awareness of themes and attitudes;

2 recognizes and appreciates ways in which authors use language;

3 recognizes and appreciates ways in which writers achieve their effects, particularly in how the work is structured and in its characterization;

4 can write imaginatively in exploring and developing ideas so as to communicate a sensitive and informed personal response to what is read.

Much of what is said in the section **Writing essays in an examination** (below) is relevant here, but for coursework essays you have the advantage of plenty of time to prepare your work – so take advantage of it.

There is no substitute for arguing, discussing and talking about a question on a particular text or theme. Your teacher should give you plenty of opportunity for this in the classroom. Listening to what others say about a subject often opens up for you new ways to look at and respond to it. The same can be said for reading about a topic. Be careful not to copy down slavishly what others say and write. Jot down notes then go away and think about what you have heard, read and written. Make more notes of your own and then start to clarify your own thoughts, feelings and emotions on the subject about which you are writing. Most students make the mistake of doing their coursework essays in a rush – you have time so use it.

Take a great deal of care in planning your work. From all your notes, write a rough draft and then start the task of really perfecting it.

1 Look at your arrangement of paragraphs, is there a logical development of thought or argument? Do the paragraphs need rearranging in order? Does the first or last sentence of any paragraph need redrafting in order to provide a sensible link with the preceding or next paragraph?

2 Look at the pattern of sentences within each paragraph. Are your thoughts and ideas clearly developed and expressed? Have you used any quotations, paraphrases, or references to incidents to support your opinions and ideas? Are those references relevant and apt, or just 'padding'?

3 Look at the words you have used. Try to avoid repeating words in close proximity one to another. Are the words you have used to comment on the text being studied the most appropriate and effective, or just the first ones you thought of?

4 Check your spelling and punctuation.

5 Now write a final draft, the quality of which should reflect the above considerations.

Writing essays in an examination
Read the question. Identify the key words and phrases. Write them down, and as they are dealt with in your essay plan, tick them off.

Plan your essay. Spend about five minutes jotting down ideas; organize your thoughts and ideas into a logical and developing order – a structure is essential to the production of a good essay. Remember, brief, essential notes only!

Write your essay
How long should it be? There is no magic length. What you must do is answer the question set, fully and sensitively in the time allowed. You will probably have about forty minutes to answer an essay question, and within that time you should produce an essay between roughly 350 and 500 words in length. Very short answers will not do justice to the question, very long answers will probably contain much irrelevant information and waste time that should be spent on the next answer.

How much quotation? Use only that which is apt and contributes to the clarity and quality of your answer. No examiner will be impressed by 'padding'.

What will the examiners be looking for in an essay?
1 An answer to the question set, and not a prepared answer to another, albeit slightly similar question done in class.

2 A well-planned, logically structured and paragraphed essay with a beginning, middle and end.

3 Accurate references to plot, character, theme, as required by the question.

4 Appropriate, brief, and if needed, frequent quotation and references to support and demonstrate the comments that you are making in your essay.

5 Evidence that reading the text has prompted in you a personal response to it, as well as some judgment and appreciation of its literary merit.

How do you prepare to do this?
1 During your course you should write between three to five essays on each text.

2 Make good use of class discussion etc, as mentioned in a previous paragraph on page 73.

3 Try to see a live performance of a play. It may help to see a film of a play or book, though be aware that directors sometimes leave out episodes, change their order, or worse, add episodes that are not in the original – so be very careful. In the end, there is no substitute for **reading and studying** the text!

Try the following exercises without referring to any notes or text.

1 Pick a character from your text.

2 Make a list of his/her qualities – both positive and negative ones, or aspects that you cannot quite define. Jot down single words to describe each quality. If you do not know the word you want, use a thesaurus, but use it in conjunction with a dictionary and make sure you are fully aware of the meaning of each word you use.

3 Write a short sentence which identifies one or more places in the text where you think each quality is demonstrated.

4 Jot down any brief quotation, paraphrase of conversation or outline of an incident which shows that quality.

5 Organize the list. Identify groupings which contrast the positive and negative aspects of character.

6 Write a description of that character which makes full use of the material you have just prepared.

7 What do you think of the character you have just described? How has he/she reacted to and coped with the pressures of the other characters, incidents, and the setting of the story? Has he/she changed in any way? In no more than 100 words, including 'evidence' taken from the text, write a balanced assessment of the character, and draw some conclusions.

You should be able to do the above without notes, and without the text, unless you are to take an examination which allows the use of plain texts. In plain text examinations you are allowed to take in a copy of your text. It must be without notes, either your own or the publisher's. The intention is to enable you to consult a text in the examination so as to confirm memory of detail, thus enabling a candidate to quote and refer more accurately in order to illustrate his/her views that more effectively. Examiners will expect a high standard of accurate reference, quotation and comment in a plain text examination.

Sitting the examination

You will have typically between two and five essays to write and you will have roughly 40 minutes, on average, to write each essay.

On each book you have studied, you should have a choice of doing at least one out of two or three essay titles set.

1   **Before sitting the exam**, make sure you are completely clear in your mind that you know exactly how many questions you must answer, which sections of the paper you must tackle, and how many questions you may, or must, attempt on any one book or in any one section of the paper. If you are not sure, ask your teacher.

2   **Always read the instructions** given at the top of your examination paper. They are

there to help you. Take your time, and try to relax – panicking will not help.

3 **Be very clear about timing, and organizing your time.**

(a) Know how long the examination is.
(b) Know how many questions you must do.
(c) Divide (b) into (a) to work out how long you may spend on each question. (Bear in mind that some questions may attract more marks, and should therefore take proportionately more time.)
(d) Keep an eye on the time, and do not spend more than you have allowed for any one question.
(e) If you have spare time at the end you can come back to a question and do more work on it.
(f) Do not be afraid to jot down notes as an aid to memory, but do cross them out carefully after use – a single line will do!

4 **Do not rush the decision** as to which question you are going to answer on a particular text.

(a) Study each question carefully.
(b) Be absolutely sure what each one is asking for.
(c) Make your decision as to which you will answer.

5 **Having decided which question** you will attempt:

(a) jot down the key points of the actual question – use single words or short phrases;
(b) think about how you are going to arrange your answer. Five minutes here, with some notes jotted down will pay dividends later;
(c) write your essay, and keep an eye on the time!

6 **Adopt the same approach** for all questions. Do write answers for the maximum number of questions you are told to attempt. One left out will lose its proportion of the total marks. Remember also, you will never be awarded extra marks, over and above those already allocated, if you write an extra long essay on a particular question.

7 **Do not waste time** on the following:

(a) an extra question – you will get no marks for it;
(b) worrying about how much anyone else is writing, they can't help you!
(c) relaxing at the end with time to spare – you do not have any. Work up to the very moment the invigilator tells you to stop writing. Check and recheck your work, including spelling and punctuation. Every single mark you gain helps, and that last mark might tip the balance between success and failure – the line has to be drawn somewhere.

8 **Help the examiner.**

(a) Do not use red or green pen or pencil on your paper. Examiners usually annotate your script in red and green, and if you use the same colours it will cause unnecessary confusion.
(b) Leave some space between each answer or section of an answer. This could also help you if you remember something you wish to add to your answer when you are checking it.
(c) Number your answers as instructed. If it is question 3 you are doing, do not label it 'C'.
(d) Write neatly. It will help you to communicate effectively with the examiner who is trying to read your script.

Glossary of literary terms

Mere knowledge of the words in this list or other specialist words used when studying literature is not sufficient. You must know when to use a particular term, and be able to describe what it contributes to that part of the work which is being discussed.

For example, merely to label something as being a metaphor does not help an examiner or teacher to assess your response to the work being studied. You must go on to analyse what the literary device contributes to the work. Why did the author use a metaphor at all? Why not some other literary device? What extra sense of feeling or meaning does the metaphor convey to the reader? How effective is it in supporting the author's intention? What was the author's intention, as far as you can judge, in using that metaphor?

Whenever you use a particular literary term you must do so with a purpose and that purpose usually involves an explanation and expansion upon its use. Occasionally you will simply use a literary term 'in passing', as, for example, when you refer to the 'narrator' of a story as opposed to the 'author' – they are not always the same! So please be sure that you understand both the meaning and purpose of each literary term you employ.

This list includes only those words which we feel will assist in helping you to understand the major concepts in play and novel construction. It makes no attempt to be comprehensive. These are the concepts which examiners frequently comment upon as being inadequately grasped by many students. Your teacher will no doubt expand upon this list and introduce you to other literary devices and words within the context of the particular work/s you are studying – the most useful place to experience and explore them and their uses.

Plot This is the plan or story of a play or novel. Just as a body has a skeleton to hold it together, so the plot forms the 'bare bones' of the work of literature in play or novel form. It is however, much more than this. It is arranged in time, so one of the things which encourages us to continue reading is to see what happens next. It deals with causality, that is how one event or incident causes another. It has a sequence, so that in general, we move from the beginning through to the end.

Structure The arrangement and interrelationship of parts in a play or novel are obviously bound up with the plot. An examination of how the author has structured his work will lead us to consider the function of, say, the 43 letters which are such an important part of *Pride and Prejudice*. We would consider the arrangement of the time-sequence in *Wuthering Heights* with its 'flashbacks' and their association with the different narrators of the story. In a play we would look at the scene divisions and how different events are placed in a relationship so as to produce a particular effect; where soliloquies occur so as to inform the audience of a character's innermost emotions and feelings. Do be aware that great works of fiction are not just simply thrown together by their authors. We study a work in detail, admiring its parts and the intricacies of its structure. The reason for a work's greatness has to do with the genius of its author and the care of its construction. Ultimately, though, we do well to remember that it is the work as a whole that we have to judge, not just the parts which make up that whole.

Narrator   A narrator tells or relates a story. In *Wuthering Heights* various characters take on the task of narrating the events of the story: Cathy, Heathcliff, etc, as well as being, at other times, central characters taking their part in the story. Sometimes the author will be there, as it were, in person, relating and explaining events. The method adopted in telling the story relates very closely to style and structure.

Style   The manner in which something is expressed or performed, considered as separate from its intrinsic content or meaning. It might well be that a lyrical, almost poetical style will be used, for example concentrating on the beauties and contrasts of the natural world as a foil to the narration of the story and creating emotions in the reader which serve to heighten reactions to the events being played out on the page. It might be that the author uses a terse, almost staccato approach to the conveyance of his story. There is no simple route to grasping the variations of style which are to be found between different authors or indeed within one novel. The surest way to appreciate this difference is to read widely and thoughtfully and to analyse and appreciate the various strategies which an author uses to command our attention.

Character   A person represented in a play or story. However, the word also refers to the combination of traits and qualities distinguishing the individual nature of a person or thing. Thus, a characteristic is one such distinguishing quality: in *Pride and Prejudice*, the pride and prejudices of various characters are central to the novel, and these characteristics which are associated with Mr Darcy, Elizabeth, and Lady Catherine in that novel, enable us to begin assessing how a character is reacting to the surrounding events and people. Equally, the lack of a particular trait or characteristic can also tell us much about a character.

Character development   In *Pride and Prejudice*, the extent to which Darcy's pride, or Elizabeth's prejudice is altered, the recognition by those characters of such change, and the events of the novel which bring about the changes are central to any exploration of how a character develops, for better or worse.

Irony   This is normally taken to be the humorous or mildly sarcastic use of words to imply the opposite of what they say. It also refers to situations and events and thus you will come across references such as prophetic, tragic, and dramatic irony.

Dramatic irony   This occurs when the implications of a situation or speech are understood by the audience but not by all or some of the characters in the play or novel. We also class as ironic words spoken innocently but which a later event proves either to have been mistaken or to have prophesied that event. When we read in the play *Macbeth*:

> *Macbeth*
> Tonight we hold a solemn supper, sir,
> And I'll request your presence.

> *Banquo*
> Let your highness
> Command upon me, to the which my duties
> Are with a most indissoluble tie
> Forever knit.

we, as the audience, will shortly have revealed to us the irony of Macbeth's words. He does not expect Banquo to attend the supper as he plans to have Banquo murdered before the supper occurs. However, what Macbeth does not know is the prophetic irony of Banquo's response. His 'duties. . . a most indissoluble tie' will be fulfilled by his appearance at the supper as a ghost – something Macbeth certainly did not forsee or welcome, and which Banquo most certainly did not have in mind!

Tragedy   This is usually applied to a play in which the main character, usually a person of importance and outstanding personal qualities, falls to disaster through the combination of personal failing and circumstances with which he cannot deal. Such tragic happenings may also be central to a novel. In *The Mayor of Casterbridge*, flaws in Henchard's character are partly responsible for his downfall and eventual death.

In Shakespeare's plays, *Macbeth* and *Othello*, the tragic heroes from which the two plays take their names, are both highly respected and honoured men who have proven their outstanding personal qualities. Macbeth, driven on by his ambition and that of his very determined wife, kills his king. It leads to civil war in his country, to his own eventual downfall and death, and to his wife's suicide. Othello, driven to an insane jealousy by the cunning of his lieutenant, Iago, murders his own innocent wife and commits suicide.

Satire   Where topical issues, folly or evil are held up to scorn by means of ridicule and irony – the satire may be subtle or openly abusive.

In *Animal Farm*, George Orwell used the rebellion of the animals against their oppressive owner to satirize the excesses of the Russian revolution at the beginning of the 20th century. It would be a mistake, however, to see the satire as applicable only to that event. There is a much wider application of that satire to political and social happenings both before and since the Russian revolution and in all parts of the world.

Images   An image is a mental representation or picture. One that constantly recurs in *Macbeth* is clothing, sometimes through double meanings of words: 'he seems rapt withal', 'Why do you dress me in borrowed robes?', 'look how our partner's rapt', 'Like our strange garments, cleave not to their mould', 'Whiles I stood rapt in the wonder of it', 'which would be worn now in their newest gloss', 'Was the hope drunk Wherein you dressed yourself?', 'Lest our old robes sit easier than our new.', 'like a giant's robe upon a dwarfish thief'. All these images serve to highlight and comment upon aspects of Macbeth's behaviour and character. In Act 5, Macbeth the loyal soldier who was so honoured by his king at the start of the play, struggles to regain some small shred of his self-respect. Three times he calls to Seyton for his armour, and finally moves toward his destiny with the words 'Blow wind, come wrack, At least we'll die with harness on our back' – his own armour, not the borrowed robes of a king he murdered.

Do remember that knowing a list of images is not sufficient. You must be able to interpret them and comment upon the contribution they make to the story being told.

Theme   A unifying idea, image or motif, repeated or developed throughout a work.

In *Pride and Prejudice*, a major theme is marriage. During the course of the novel we are shown various views of and attitudes towards marriage. We actually witness the relationships of four different couples through their courtship, engagement and eventual marriage. Through those events and the examples presented to us in the novel of other already married couples, the author engages in a thorough exploration of the theme.

This list is necessarily short. There are whole books devoted to the explanation of literary terms. Some concepts, like style, need to be experienced and discussed in a group setting with plenty of examples in front of you. Others, such as dramatic irony, need keen observation from the student and a close knowledge of the text to appreciate their significance and existence. All such specialist terms are well worth knowing. But they should be used only if they enable you to more effectively express your knowledge and appreciation of the work being studied.

Titles in the series